I0568753

1861 - 2011, 150 YEARS WITH JOHNNY REB & BILLY YANKEE

Many of us when we think of the words "civil war" one has in mind the war between the southerners and northerners, soldiers in blue or gray wearing floppy berrets and armed with muskets and swords. Men organized in battalions and regiments led by legendary generals such as Ulysses S. Grant, Robert Edward Lee, "Stonewall" Jackson, Sheridan and others. The more knowledgeable know the names of the most important battles such as Antietam, Fredericksburg, Gettysburg, Vicksburg, Chickamauga, Atlanta and also the fact that the southerners surrender was signed at Appomattox. Some (not many) have also knowledge of the name of the various units involved in the clashes such as the Irish Brigade, the Iron Brigade, the Cavalry of Stuart and Mosby as well as the Brigade of Stonewall the 20th Maine, etc.

All these interesting facts and stories have been captured and facilitated by an impressive set of publications, studies and research that have the theme of the American Civil War. The American Civil War which occurred 150 years ago, is one of the largest events in American history, and is still very topical and generates keen interest. It is an event that continues to affect the way we think, we conduct politics, the formulation of laws etc.

1861-2011, 150 ANNI CON JOHNNY REB & BILLY YANKEE

Molti di noi, quando pensano alle parole "guerra civile", hanno bene in mente che si sta parlando della guerra fra sudisti e nordisti americani, soldati in blu o in grigio con indosso berrettini flosci, armati di moschetti e spade. Uomini inquadrati in battaglioni e reggimenti, guidati da mitici generali come Ulisse Grant, Robert Edward Lee, "Stonewall" Jakson, Sheridan e altri. I più informati conoscono i nomi delle più importanti battaglie: Antietam, Fredericksburg, Gettysburg, Vicksburg, Chickamauga, Atlanta, fino alla resa sudista firmata ad Appomattox.

Alcuni hanno anche familiarità con i nomi delle grandi unità impegnate negli scontri: la Irish Brigade, la Iron Brigade, I cavalleggeri di Stuart e di Mosby ed ancora la brigata di Stonewall, il 20° Maine ecc.

Tutto ciò è stato facilitato da un'impressionante messe di pubblicazioni, studi e ricerche che hanno per tema la guerra civile americana. Argomento sempre di moda e di vivo interesse, specialmente, come è ovvio, negli Stati Uniti, dove il più grande evento nella storia americana, la guerra civile appunto, nei suoi aspetti militari e non, continua a condizionare il modo di vivere, di pensare, di fare politica, di suggerirne le leggi in modo irrevocabile. E' cosi da 150 anni; probabilmente lo sarà per sempre.

"I had to go. A spirit in my feet said 'Go,' and I went." (M.Brady)

CONTENTS - INDICE:

A Ermanno Albertelli con stima e amicizia !

▲ Riley US officer
The only information related this image is : "Riley" a title from unverified information on negative sleeve of LC Civil War shot collection. Probably this is the name of this officer in his dark blue double-breasted frock coat and regulation blue sky trousers.

Riley un ufficiale nordista
L'unica informazione disponibile su questa bella immagine della Libreria del Congresso è il titolo "Riley". Probabilmente si tratta del cognome dell'ufficiale raffigurato che indossa la tenuta regolamentare composta dalla giacca blu scuro in doppio petto e i pantaloni azzurro cielo.

LUCA STEFANO CRISTINI

AMERICAN CIVIL WAR
150 YEARS & 150 PHOTOS

GLI UOMINI CHE FECERO LA GUERRA CIVILE AMERICANA - 150 ANNI E 150 FOTO

WAR IN COLOUR 002

SOLDIERSHOP PUBLISHING

AUTHORS - AUTORI:

Luca Stefano Cristini, is an Italian leading historical hautor and illustrator. Specialising in medieval and Renaissance period. He is author of about twenty books for Soldiershop Publishing, Isomedia, Albertelli (Tuttostoria), and De Agostini Publishing.

Luca Stefano Cristini, appassionato da sempre di storia militare. Dirige da diversi anni riviste nazionali specializzate di carattere storico uniformologico. Ha collaborato con l'editore Albertelli e la De Agostini. Ha al suo attivo una ventina di libri di storia e uniformologia di cui cura sia il testo che le illustrazioni.

Franco Andreone, Australian of Italian origins, passionate about military history and our faithful English translator of the texts and captions for our book.

Franco Andreone, australiano di origine italiane, appassionato da sempre di storia militare è il nostro fedele traduttore per i testi e le didascalie in inglese dei nostri libri.

PUBLISHING'S NOTE - NOTE EDITORIALI

WAR IN COLOUR

This line realizes books of military historical subjects mainly using the re-coloration of old and rare photos in black and white, offering in this way an interesting new life to faded images. This series covers a huge range of world conflicts from the Crimean war through to World War Two.

◀ **Previous page: Petersburg, Virginia. Group of Federal generals: W.S. Hancock, J. Gibbon, F.C. Barlow and W.Birney.** Winfield Scott Hancock (February 14, 1824 – February 9, 1886) was a career U.S. Army officer and the Democratic nominee for President of the United States in 1880 (later win by the republican James A. Garfield). He served in the Mexican-American War and as a Union general in the American Civil War. Known to his Army colleagues as "Hancock the Superb", he was famous in particular for his personal leadership at the Battle of Gettysburg in 1863. One military historian wrote, "No other Union general at Gettysburg dominated men by the sheer force of their presence more completely than Hancock. In this image Hancock seated, is surrounded by three of his division commanders: Francis C. Barlow at left, David B. Birney in the centre, and John Gibbon at right during the Wilderness campaign.

Pagina prec.: Petersburg, Virginia. Foto di gruppo di generali unionisti: W.S. Hancock, J. Gibbon, F.C. Barlow e W.Birney. Winfield Scott Hancock (1824 –1886) fu uno dei più famosi generali nordisti della Guerra. Dopo la Guerra divenne famoso per essere candidato del partito democratico alle elezioni presidenziali del 1880 poi perse a vantaggio del repubblicano James A.Garfield. Hancock servì nella Guerra messicana e nella Guerra Civile si distinse particolarmente a Gettysburg. Il suo eroico atteggiamento fu celebrato da numerosi storici e testimoni. Tuttavia i colleghi lo chiamarono sempre "Hancock il superbo". In questa immagine lo vediamo seduto attorniato dal suo staff. Da sinistra a destra: Francis C. Barlow, David B. Birney e John Gibbon durante la campagna di Wilderness.

▶ **Washington, District of Columbia. Men of 3d Reg. Massachusetts Heavy Artillery by Columbiad guns, Fort Totten.**
Washington, Dis. Columbia. Uomini del 3° Reg. Massachusetts Heavy Artillery con cannoni Columbiad, Fort Totten.

ISBN: 978-88-9327-086-1   3rd edition: June 2016
Title: **AMERICAN CIVIL WAR - 150 YEARS & 150 PHOTOS (WAR IN COLOUR 002)** by Luca Stefano Cristini.
Editor: SOLDIERSHOP PUBLISHING. Cover & Art Design: Luca S. Cristini. Illustrations restored & re-colored by Luca S.Cristini. Correzioni bozze di Monica Balzi. Franco Andreone ha curato le parti in inglese.
The publisher wishes to thanks especially the honorable Library of Congress for the great part of the images used in this book. Where otherwise indicated the original images are of Library of Congress (LC).

In cover : **Maj. H. W. Sawyer and staff at Camp Stoneman District of Columbia 1862 about.**
Printing by/Stampato da ColorArt di Rodengo Saiano (BS) Italy.

O CAPTAIN ! MY CAPTAIN
150 YEARS AGO, THE AMERICAN CIVIL WAR

"*A*nd that the Government of the people, by the people, for the people, not to disappear from the Earth". So ended the famous Gettysburg Address pronounced on 19th November 1863 by a beaming Abraham Lincoln, President of the United States on the battlefield of Gettysburg. Gettysburg was one of the bloodiest and decisive battles of the American civil war which was won by the Union troops led by General Meade. This major victory laid the groundwork for the final victory which took place only two years later.

This memorable text, extolled the gigantic figure of President Lincoln, one of the greatest that the Union has had in its secular history. Its echo resounded throughout the nation, wounded by years of heavy and terrible conflict. Among the greatest mentors of that speech was Walt Whitman, contemporary American poet who dedicated to Lincoln his poem with the famous verses: "O Captain! My Captain! Our tremendous journey is finished …" words made famous by the movie Dead Poets Society by the director Peter Weir.

The same Whitman in Drum Rolls after weeping for the death of Lincoln on the tragic night of 14th April 1865 at the Ford's Theatre, enhances the Union's victory that finally ended the carnage: "Rejoice, o beaches, and play, or bells!". All this began in the beautiful and fatal spring of 1861...

▼ **The Gettysburg Address** was delivered by Lincoln on the afternoon of Thursday, November 19, 1863, at the dedication of the Soldiers' National Cemetery in Gettysburg, Pennsylvania. Ancient print (LC).

Il Gettysburg Address venne pronunciato da Lincoln nel pomeriggio del 19 novembre 1863, in occasione dell'inaugurazione del cimitero di guerra nazionale di Gettysburg, Pennsylvania. Stampa dell'epoca (LC).

I ASK FOR THE HONOUR OF FIRING FIRST!

Edmund Ruffin of the class of 1794, controversial character, noteworthy secessionist, farmer, slaveholder, soldier and dedicated political activist, was musing in the mirror one warm day in April of 1861 sees the reflection of a face which is dry with long hair. His inseparable shotgun, mainly used to protect his land against bears and wolves, is supported nearby and, this time will be aimed at a target more epic that will project him into history.

When it became clear in the young American nation that hostilities between the North and South was now a matter of hours rather than days, the Virginian Ruffin, took with him a few belongings and his rifle, departed full of enthusaism for the mission and headed for Charleston, South Carolina. Here the secessionist rebels surrounded Fort Sumter, a fortified Island full of unionist cannons placed in the southern Bay of the city and asked the loyalist Colonel Robert Anderson to surrender. At 3:20 a.m. on 12th April 1861, the Confederates in order to convince him to surrender, informed Anderson that they would open fire within an hour. At 4:30 a.m. on the same day, a single broadside of mortars was fired from the nearby Fort Johnson falling on Fort Sumter.

This was the beginning of the bombing, with 43 mortars firing on the Union's fort, a well known episode in the American civil war. All this happened just moments after Edmund Ruffin fired the first shot of the war against the same stronghold. Anderson did not respond to this attack until 7:00 a.m. Then began a frenzied counter bombardment. Once all the shots had been fired, the Fort surrendered and Ruffin also gained the honour of being one of the first to enter the conquered Fort Sumter.

June 1865, after four years of conflict, after the surrender of Robert E. Lee, Commander of the southern army at Appomattox Court House, the fiery southerner Ruffin, maybe back in front of his mirror, saw him leave Charleston, wrote in his diary his last words of deep hatred towards his Yankee enemy. Shortly after, Ruffin "dressed" with his beloved Confederate flag took his life with a gunshot to the head. This man had the singular fate of starting and in some way participating at the end of the American civil war.

Ruffin, however, is just one of many that made this war.

In 1861 the North and South together had about 31 million people.
The American civil war was one of the first conflicts which was photographed. Some experimental *"dagherro types"* were made in the previous war against Mexico at the end of the 1840s, but they were few and vague images. However it was during the Crimean War of 1854, that warfare was captured on camera by the Englishman Roger Fenton, the first true photo-journalist of history. However, the art of photography in those years developed in leaps and bounds, and only a few years later: Brady, O'Sullivan, Gardner and others took with extreme care clear images of the great American conflict.

They managed to capture not only the aforementioned Ruffin but also important personalities such as Lincoln, Davis, Grant, Lee, Jackson, Mosby, McLellan and a myriad of other senior officers and politicians, but also captains, sergeants, privates, black slaves, women, workers and sailors. Battlegrounds, railways, ports, towns destroyed by the conflict and countless "landscapes" of this time were also photographed.

These beautiful gray or sephia images loaded with character have been re-interpreted by us using the colours likely for the uniforms, faces and landscapes of that time and make up the lion's share of this publication.

▲ **Edmund Ruffin (1794 –1865)** was a farmer and slaveholder, a soldier, and after an ardent supporter of the Confederacy and a longstanding enemy of the North. Because of his strong secessionist views and the widely held belief that he fired the first shot of the Battle of Fort Sumter, Ruffin is credited as "firing the first shot of the Civil War."

Edmund Ruffin (1794-1865) fu un agricoltore, schiavista e soldato, più tardi fervente supporter della Confederazione sudista e mitico nemico del Nord. A causa del suo accesso secessionismo e dei suoi punti di vista radicali, durante l'assedio di Fort Sumter gli venne consesso l'onore di sparare il primo colpo della Guerra Civile.

▶ **The fall of General Reynolds** at Gettysburg. He was killed at the very start of the battle the July 1, 1863 by a shot of a Confederate sharpshooter.

La morte del generale Reynolds a Gettysburg. Egli venne colpito da un cecchino sudista all'inizio della battaglia IL 1° luglio 1863.

THE PHOTOGRAPHERS OF THE WAR

MATHEW BRADY (1822 – 1896)
"I had to go. A spirit in my feet told me to go, so I went"

Mathew B. Brady was born in Warren County, a suburb near New York City to a family of Irish descent. In his early 20s he had his own photographic studio in New York where he shot portraits on daguerreotype and he had considerable success thanks to his capabilities. The development of the photographic technique occurred during those years with the switching over from the complicated daguerrotype to the calotype, followed by the ambrotype, to the ferrotype and finally to that of plates.

Those were the years in which the photographic fashion of "cartes de visite" also became popular, the type of portrait studies which was launched in Paris. These were the major commissions for the Brady studio.

His fame however came mainly from his activity in the years immediately preceding and during the American civil war. At the end of the war, the general public became tired of the war and lost interest in seeing photos associated with the war and this fact made Brady's popularity decline drastically. At the beginning of the conflict Brady left his tranquil photographic studio and moved to the battlefields hence his saying "I had to go. A spirit in my feet told me to go, so I went". It was at that time a titanic undertaking, bearing in mind that there were no small modern digital cameras. In 1861, the difficulty of bringing the bulky and heavy wooden equipment to the field accompanied by a series of bulky accessories was very problematic.

Tied to this task was the high risk faced by these photographers and history demonstrates how many war photo-journalists died. For example, reference can be made to Robert Capa (who died in the first Indochina war) and Gerda Taro (who died in the war of Spain). Brady personally made his first shots at the battle of Bull Run in 1861 with projectiles whistling close by. Risks aside, the work excited him and it earned him a lot of money, so much that he decided to hire staff. Some of these hired photographers became important names in the history of photo-journalism. Among them were Alexander Gardner, James Gardner, Timothy H. O'Sullivan, William Pywell, George N. Barnard, Thomas C. Roche, and many others. All these provided important imagery and their activities were organized and coordinated from Washington.

From his studio emerged famous pictures and images that are largely preserved today by the United States Library of Congress. For the first time in the history of wars, there were photographs depicting corpses of soldiers fallen in battle. But the main subjects were of the senior officers, both northerners and southerners, for example Ulysses S. Grant and Robert E. Lee. These subjects were shot in various settings, under tents, near cannons or mounted on horses. On several occasions Brady also photographed the Union President, Abraham Lincoln, these portraits have become classic iconography of this great President. It is estimated that throughout the war Brady produced no less than 10,000 prints. Mathew Brady is considered by far the most important photo-journalists of the conflict, and one of the greatest photographers of all time, together with his father and alongside Roger Fenton (who photographed the Crimean War).

In addition to his images of war, Brady was famous for the long series of portraits of celebrities. From American Presidents, intellectuals and great men of the time such as Mark Twain, Edgar Allan Poe, Thomas Edison to almost mythical characters such as General Custer, Kit Carson or Garibaldi. After the war, a series of unfortunate circumstances almost reduced him to poverty. Tired, depressed and widowed, Brady died almost forgotten in 1896. Insomuch that there was not even enough money to pay the funeral, the veterans of the 7th New York infantry regiment held a ceremony. His body rests today in the Congressional Cemetery in Washington. The only limitation that his and his colleagues' images had was imposed by the technique available at that time. They could not take pictures of people or things in motion, as this would create a heavy blurring in the photographs.

▲ **Mathew B. Brady (1822-1896)** was born in Warren County, New York and was considered with Roger Fenton one of the father of photojournalism. He was the greatest American photo-historian of the 19th century, and undoubtedly Abraham Lincoln's favorite photographer.

Mathew B. Brady (1822-1896) nacque a Warren County, New York. E' considerato insieme a Roger Fenton uno dei padri del moderno fotogiornalismo. Fu il più grande fotoreporter americano del 19° secolo e senza dubbio il più amato dal presidente Lincoln.

◄ **Roger Fenton (1819 – 1869)** was a pioneering British photographer, one of the first war photographers. Very famous his several shots of Crimean war. In the image his collaborator Marcus Sparling seated on Fenton's photographic van, Crimea, 1855.

Roger Fenton (1819 – 1869) fu uno dei primi pionieri della fotografia di guerra. Celebri i suoi scatti della guerra di Crimea, di poco precedente la Guerra civile. Nell'immagine il suo assistente M.Sparling sul carro da ripresa in Crimea nel 1855.

► **Musket infantry of ACW.** Moschetto da fanteria. Coll. autore

TIMOTHY O'SULLIVAN (1840-1882)

O'Sullivan was born in 1840 in Ireland. His family immigrated to the United States and settled in New York. At eighteen years old, Timothy began working as an apprentice at the studio of Mathew Brady, with whom he shared his Irish origins. O'Sullivan was among the first employees sent to the front by Brady to document photographically the conduct of the conflict. He demonstrated immediately to be a talented photographer, especially for his skill in making the most of the features of the cameras of that era. Due to the limitations of the technology, he focused mainly on static images and footage of the battlefield immediately after the cessation of fighting, capturing scenes of great drama, especially regarding the details of the fallen. Alongside him there was also Alexander Gardner another historic photographer of the American civil war. In 1863, O'Sullivan separated from Brady and continued filming the war in collaboration with Gardner, competing with their former employer. In the famous Gardner's 'Photographic Sketch Book of the War', the first collection of 100 pictures of war included forty four photos taken by O'Sullivan. After the war, he got important commissions for scientific and geographic topics. Between 1867 to 1869, he was the official photographer of the scientific expedition entitled "United States Geological Exploration of the 40th Parallel", during which he photographed the mines of the Comstock Lode, using artificial magnesium lighting, a revolutionary technique for that period. In 1870 he worked as a reporter to cover the construction of the Panama Canal.

In 1871 he participated in a geographic expedition that involved the documentation of the American landscape and shot on these occasions some wonderful photos of some American Indian tribes the Navajos and Ute.

He also shot other subjects such as the Central Pacific Railway. O'Sullivan photographed canyons, lakes and mountains of America with expertise and artistry that lead him to be appointed head of the photographic sector of the U.S. Treasury. Sick with tuberculosis he died at the age of forty two in New York on 14th January 1882.

ALEXANDER GARDNER (1821 - 1882)

Curiously, after the Irish born Brady and O'Sullivan, the third great photographer of the American civil war is not. Indeed, Gardner was born in Scotland and moved when he was thirty five to the United States in 1856, with the aim of developing his profession as a photographer. In New York he came into contact with Brady and soon became one of his main collaborators. His contemporary friendship with Allan Pinkerton (who was head of an intelligence service that later became the American secret service) opened many opportunities for work. As for the two afore-mentioned, Gardner also owes his fame to the photographs taken during the American civil war, but he was also known for the various shots of the American President Abraham Lincoln, in addition to images of the execution of the conspirators for the assassination of the President. Thanks to all these contacts, Gardner became the personal photographer for General George B. McClellan, Commander in Chief of the army of the Potomac. At this point, the Scottish photographer was a mature veteran. As a result he separated from Brady and opened up his own studio in Washington with his brother James as well as many former employees of Brady. Meanwhile Gardner increased his photographic profile by shooting the famous battles of Antietam (1862), Gettysburg (July 1863) and the siege of Petersburg (June 1864-April 1865). At the end of the war, in 1866 he published a photographic book on the civil war (Gardner's Photographic sketch book of the war) composed of approximately 100 photographs chosen among the best pictures of the war. The images published were not all his work but are the work of various photographers of his studio such as T. O'Sullivan, James F. Gibson, John Reekie, William Pywell, James Gardner (his brother), John Wood, George N. Barnard, David Knox and David Woodbury among others. After the war, as with O'Sullivan, Gardner received the assignment to photograph American Indians who came to Washington to discuss peace treaties. He lived in Washington until his death in 1882.

The 'scandal' of the created scene

In 1961, some scholars examining the vast photographic work of Gardner realised that the famous photographer, at least on one occasion, had 'created' the scene. The journalist Frederic Ray realised that a corpse of a southern soldier at Gettysburg with his rifle in fact appeared in two different photos. What had happened? Simple, Gardner with the help of his assistants Timothy O'Sullivan and James Gibson had dragged the body of a southern sniper 40 meters away from the exact point where this person had died and placed him in a more photogenic location near the famous Devil's Den. This was considered quite scandalous practice in the early years of photography, and to some extent controversial even today.

WILLIAM REDISH PYWELL (1843 - 1887)

American photographer, Pywell like many others began his apprenticeship with Matthew Brady and Alexander Gardner. With the latter he collaborated on the famous book published by Gardner in 1866: "Photographic sketch book of the war". After the war, he undertook geographic photographic shoots and travelled with George Custer as official photographer in the Yellowstone Expedition of 1873.

JAMES F. GIBSON (1825-1905)

Gibson was born in New York City. He knew Brady and worked in his studio. He was known for his shots of General McClellan during the peninsula campaign, the battle of Seven Days, Gaines ' Mill and Malvern Hill. He died in 1905.

THOMAS C. ROCHE (1826-1895)

Photographer following the army of James. When talking about Roche one needs to refer to a curious anecdote which highlights his courage. One day while he was photographing in the midst of a battle, an artillery projectile exploded nearby, which fortunately did not wound him, but after the dust settled, Roche planted his camera in the middle of the crater caused by the recent explosion and continued photographing as if nothing had happened.

GEORGE S. COOK (1819-1902)

▲ At left "The home of a Rebel Sharpshooter, Gettysburg", the famous created scene, present in Alexander Gardner's Photographic Sketch Book of the Civil War. At right, the real position of the confederate died soldier.

A sinistra la foto incriminata. Gardner spostò il soldato, visibile nella foto a destra per migliorare la drammaticità dell'immagine. Lo scandalo venne scoperto solo nel 1961.

▼ Colt Navy replica. Author collection.
Colt Navy replica. Collezione autore.

The best known photographer of the Confederate was George Cook. He was born in Stamford, Connecticut, in 1819. He moved first to New Orleans where he studied art and became a professional painter. In 1842, he discovered photography with the arrival of the daguerreotype in America. Later, with his family he moved to Charleston, South Carolina where he came into contact with the realities of war (which began in that city). A final and definitive transfer led him to the southern capital of Richmond, Virginia where he shot the most comprehensive collection of photographs of that city. He died on 27th November 1902. Famous for his pictures of Fort Sumter. Unfortunately, most of Cook's photographs were lost in a fire in 1864. Cook among other things was also known as the Brady of the South.

▼ **George Smith Cook** was a prominent early American photographer. The most famous in the Confederate field. For this reason is also named: " The Southern Mathew Brady" ! in this image he is in the middle.

George Smith Cook fu un valente fotoreporter dell'era pionieristica americana, il più noto nel campo confederato, tanto da essere soprannominato il Brady del Sud ! nella foto appare in mezzo a due suoi amici e colleghi.

THE CIVIL WAR

In the 1850s the United States was a nation booming and expanding, they were involved and engaged in the conquest of endless territories to the West, bringing them in contact with the Pacific Ocean. In the 1840s, the US easily took control of the territories previously under Mexico (California, New Mexico, Arizona and Texas) and forced into small reserves the American Indian tribes. The United States quickly became a powerful and enormous country with great resources and potential, but still with a fledgling and fragile internal structure and institutions this soon led to a military confrontation. With the election of President Abraham Lincoln in 1860, one of the fiercest opponents of slavery and a person strongly aligned with the industrial North, a rift emerged between the two worlds of the north and south. These two worlds had radically different views when it came to politics and economics. The American Civil War or War of Cession is still to this day a fundamental topic for American historians. Not only was this event the most grave of events for the North American nation, but also because in its interpretation, ideas and analyses are often at odds with each other and never quite defined. In fact, the major themes of the entire United States are embodied in the civil war, namely the relationship between States and Federal Government, economic development, industrialization and slavery, discussions found in the study of history, politics and military.

It is traditional to ascribe slavery and the attempt to abolish it as the main reason for the war. With the contrast between President Lincoln's desire to abolish it and the commercial need for this amongst the aristocratic southern ruling families. One of the foremost analysts of the history of the conflict was James Ford Rhodes who, with his 'History of the Civil War', while supporting the theory that slavery was one of the causes of the war, was the first to attribute the main cause to a complex antagonism between the two parties based on economic, social and political views. This hypothesis is backed up by the fact that although slavery was integrated into the social fabric of the south, it would eventually and naturally disintegrate some decades thereafter. Therefore the causes of the civil war are attributed by Rhodes to larger and more complex issues. Slavery does not provide all the answers to why this

conflict emerged. The conflict took place for several reasons, from the chauvinism and fanaticism that fatally divided the southern Johnny Reb from the northern Billy Yankee to more exquisitely political complications with the physical and geographical divide of the land and also to the American two-party system: Republicans and Democrats in the North and South.

History recounts that in February 1861, eleven Southern States united to form the "Confederation", an autonomous nation. The Confederate States of America included South Carolina, Mississippi, Florida, Alabama, Georgia, Louisiana, Texas, Virginia, Arkansas, Tennessee and North Carolina. The North did not accept this fracture and this inevitably led to the start of the conflict which was long and bloody (with 600,000 deaths), the most bloody since the Napoleonic campaigns.

The civil war was also the first modern conflict thanks to the great contribution of industry (especially in the North), the widespread use of the railway and the development of modern artillery. During the war there were also revolutionary inventions such as the submarine, the armour of the boats, the telegraph which allowed the spread of news to the enemy. All this made this war a "total war" that proved so very deadly with fighters lamenting the numerous victims of the conflict as never seen in any war before. The war ended with the announcement and inevitable victory of the Northern States, who were economically stronger. The defeat of the South led to an immediate end to slavery, which by its sudden abolition was a deadly blow to the economic sustainability of agricultural in the former confederate states. The American civil war ended with a rapid industrial explosion in the nation. Railway lines linked the two coasts, the American Indians suffered heavy losses and the last were finally smothered of their human rights. The United States, within a few decades after Appomatox, the pleasant location where Lee signed the surrender of the South in the presence of Ulysses Grant, would become one of the greatest world powers.

Italy and the USA 150 years of history

1861 is a date that historically unites Italy and the USA. Both share 150 year celebrations, in Italy's case it marks the birth of a nation. In the second case, 1861 marks the beginning of a heavy conflict which lasted four long years and which risked to "starve" the young nation on the other side of the ocean. For the many Italians living in America they have two 150th. From the American side, many Americans of Italian origin served as volunteers or served in the US army. We recall the Bersaglieri of the "Garibaldi Guard" from New York a regiment formed by many of Italian countrymen.

OH CAPITANO! MIO CAPITANO!
150 ANNI FA, LA GUERRA CIVILE AMERICANA

◄ **Drum corps, 8th New York** State Militia, Arlington, Va., June, 1861 portrait of 18 men and boys.

*Drum corps, 8° New York State Militia, Arlington, Va., Giugno 1861
Foto di gruppo di 18 soldati e ragazzi.*

▼ **Staff meeting July 1865.** Washington, District of Columbia. Brevetted Brigadier General Napoleon Bonaparte McLaughlen (seated, second from right) and staff. Photographer unknown. Napoleon Bonaparte Mclaughlin, retiring in 1882, was born in Chelsea Vermont in 1823.

1865. Washington, District of Columbia. Il brigadiere generale Napoleon Bonaparte McLaughlen (seduto, e secondo da destra) con il suo staff. Fotografo sconosciuto. Napoleon Bonaparte Mclaughlin, nacque a Chelsea Vermont nel 1823 e si ritirò nel 1882.

"..E che il governo del popolo, dal popolo, per il popolo, non scompaia dalla terra". Così si concludeva il famoso Gettysburg Address (Discorso di Gettysburg) pronunciato il 19 novembre 1863 da un raggiante Abraham Lincoln, Presidente degli Stati Uniti sul campo di battaglia di Gettysburg: una delle più sanguinose, decisive battaglie della guerra civile americana combattuta solo pochi mesi prima, e vinta dalle truppe nordiste guidate dal generale Meade.Fase importante che pose i presupposti per la definitiva vittoria finale avvenuta solo due anni dopo.

Questo memorabile testo, esaltava la gigantesca figura del presidente Lincoln, certo fra i più grandi che l'Unione abbia avuto nel corso della sua secolare storia. La sua eco risuonò per tutta la nazione, ferita da anni da un conflitto pesante e terribile. Fra i massimi mentori di quel discorso vi fu Walt Whitman, il grande poeta americano contemporaneo, che a Lincoln dedicò la poesia che esordiva con i celebri versi:"O Capitano! Mio Capitano!Il nostro viaggio tremendo è finito…" parole rese celebri dal film l'Attimo fuggente del regista Peter Weir.

Lo stesso Whitman in Rulli di tamburo, dopo aver pianto la morte di Lincoln, avvenuta nella tragica serata del 14 Aprile 1865 al Ford's Theatre, esalta finalmente la vittoria nordista che pose fine alla carneficina: "Esultate, o spiagge, e suonate, o campane!".

Tutto questo ebbe inizio nella bella e fatale primavera del 1861…

CHIEDO L'ONORE DI SPARARE PER PRIMO !

Edmund Ruffin classe 1794, controverso personaggio, secessionista degno di nota, agricoltore e schiavista, soldato e convinto attivista politico, un caldo giorno d'aprile del 1861 si osserva meditabondo allo specchio che gli rimanda la visione di un viso secco con una famigliare lunghissima capigliatura canuta. Il suo inseparabile lungo fucile da caccia, principalmente utilizzato fino ad allora per tenere lontani orsi e lupi dalle sue terre,è appoggiato lì vicino ed è stavolta destinato ad un obiettivo più epico che lo proietterà nella storia.

Quando, nella giovane nazione americana, fu a tutti chiaro che le ostilità fra Nord e Sud erano ormai questione di ore, al massimo di giorni, il virginiano Ruffin, prese con sè poche cose oltre al suo fucile e partì convinto ed entusiasta per la missione che si era prefigurato: destinazione Charleston, nella Carolina del Sud. Qui i rivoltosi secessionisti circondavano da qualche tempo Fort Sumter, un'isola fortificata unionista piena di cannoni posta nella baia della città sudista, chiedendone inutilmente la resa al suo comandante, il lealista colonnello Robert Anderson. Alle 3:20 del mattino del 12 aprile 1861, i confederati per convincerlo alla resa, informarono Anderson che avrebbero aperto il fuoco entro un'ora. Ed effettivamente alle 4:30 di quella giornata una singola bordata di mortai sparò dal vicino Fort Johnson cadendo su Fort Sumter. Questo fu l'inizio del bombardamento, operato da 43 mortai, verso il forte dell'Unione, episodio che notoriamente diede il via alla guerra di secessione americana. Tutto questo però avvenne pochi attimi dopo che fu esplosa la fucilata di Edmund Ruffin, il quale chiese e ottenne l'onore di sparare il primo colpo della guerra contro lo stesso forte. Anderson non rispose all'attacco fino alle 7:00 del mattino. A quell'ora diede inizio ad un forsennato tiro di controbatteria. Una volta terminati tutti i colpi che aveva a disposizione per i suoi cannoni il forte si arrese e qui ricomparse il nostro Ruffin che ottenne anche l'onore di entrare per primo a Fort Sumter appena conquistato.

Giugno 1865. Trascorsi i quattro anni del conflitto, dopo la resa di Robert E. Lee, comandante dell'armata sudista ad Appomattox Court House, l'ardente sudista Ruffin, forse tornato davanti al suo specchio che lo vide partire per Charleston, scrisse nel diario le sue ultime parole di odio profondo nei confronti del nemico yankee. Poco dopo, Ruffin "vestito" dell'amata bandiera confederata si tolse la vita con un colpo di pistola alla testa. Quest'uomo ebbe la singolare sorte di iniziare, e per certi versi di terminare, la guerra civile americana.

Ruffin è però solo uno dei tanti che fecero questa guerra. Nel 1861 Nord e Sud contavano insieme circa 31 milioni di

▲ Bullets of Gettysburg. Author's collection.

Palle e proiettili da moschetto trovati a Gettysburg. Collezione dell'autore.

◄ Ancient Map of Antietam battle The Battle of Antietam also known as the Battle of Sharpsburg, particularly in the South, fought on September 17, 1862 and was the first major battle in the American Civil War to take place on North field. It was also the bloodiest single-day battle in American history, with about 23,000 casualties.

Antica mappa della battaglia di Antietam. La battaglia di Antietam, chiamata di Sharpsburg dai sudisti, venne combattuta il 17 settembre 1862 e fu la prima grossa battaglia che venne combattuta sul suolo nordista. Fu anche la più sanguinosa battaglia di un giorno dell'intera guerra con oltre 23.000 perdite.

► Brady's photo outfit in front of Petersburg, Virginia.

Carro con attrezzatura fotografica di M.Brady a Petersburg, Virginia.

persone. La guerra civile americana fu uno dei primi conflitti della storia ad essere fotografato. Alcuni "dagherrotipi" sperimentali furono fatti nella precedente guerra contro il Messico, alla fine degli anni 40 del XIX secolo, ma si trattava di poche ed indefinite immagini. Il vero record spettò quindi alla guerra di Crimea del 1854, ampiamente ripresa dalle foto dell'inglese Roger Fenton, primo vero fotoreporter della storia. Tuttavia l'arte della fotografia fa in quegli anni passi da gigante, e già solo pochi anni dopo Brady, O'Sullivan, Gardner e altri, riprendono, con estrema e migliorata cura, quantità e qualità, per l'appunto il grande conflitto americano. Finiscono così sulla "gelatina" non solo il citato Ruffin, ma soprattutto Lincoln, Davis, Grant, Lee, Jackson, Mosby, Mc Lellan e miriadi di altri alti ufficiali e politici; inoltre capitani, sergenti e soldati semplici. Schiavi negri, donne, operai e marinai. Campi di battaglia, ferrovie, porti, città distrutte e infiniti "landscapes": insomma viene fotografata tutta l'America di allora ! Queste belle immagini grigie o seppiate, cariche di suggestioni sono state da noi re-interpretate con il colore che verosimilmente uniformi, visi e paesaggi del tempo dovettero avere e fanno oggi, ad un secolo e mezzo di distanza da quella sanguinosa guerra, la parte del leone in questa nostra pubblicazione.

I FOTOGRAFI DELLA GUERRA

MATTHEW BRADY (1822 –1896)

"Dovevo andare. Uno spirito nei miei piedi mi disse vai e io andai".
Matthew B. Brady nasce a Warren County, un sobborgo vicino a New York da una famiglia di origini irlandesi. Poco più che ventenne avvia un proprio studio fotografico a New York dove esegue ritratti su dagherrotipo incontrando subito un notevole successo grazie alle sue indubbie capacità. Sono anni storici per lo sviluppo della tecnica fotografica. In pochi anni si passa dal complicatissimo dagherrotipo al calotipo, seguito poi all'ambrotipo, al ferrotipo ed infine alle lastre al collodio. Sono quelli gli anni in cui negli studi fotografici esplode la moda delle "cartes de visite", tipo di ritratto lanciato negli studi parigini. Queste sono, al tempo, anche le maggiori commissioni dello studio Brady. La sua fama tuttavia gli

arriva principalmente dalla sua attività svolta negli anni immediatamente precedenti e durante la Guerra di secessione americana. Mentre negli anni successivi, il pubblico in generale, stanco della guerra, perse interesse nel vedere le foto delle guerre e la popolarità di Brady diminuì drasticamente.

All'inizio del conflitto dunque Brady lascia la tranquillità del suo studio fotografico e si trasferisce sui campi di battaglia; dirà più tardi: "Dovevo andare. Uno spirito nei miei piedi mi disse vai e io andai". Era ai tempi un'impresa titanica. Va considerato ovviamente che non c'erano ancora le moderne macchine digitali che stanno in tasca e con una buona memoria permettono di fare migliaia di foto. Nel 1861 la difficoltà di portare sul terreno le attrezzature da ripresa, costituite da pesanti fotocamere in legno di dimensioni non trascurabili, accompagnate da tutta una serie di ingombranti accessori era assai problematica.

A questo andavano uniti i rischi del mestiere e la storia dimostrerà quanti fotoreporter di guerra faranno una brutta fine. Basti pensare, una su tutti, alla coppia Robert Capa (perito nella Guerra d'Indocina) e Gerda Taro (morta nella guerra di Spagna). I suoi primi scatti, Brady li fa personalmente sul campo di battaglia di Bull Run nel 1861 con i proiettili che gli fischiano vicini. Rischi a parte, il lavoro lo entusiasma e lo fa guadagnare molto, tanto che decide di assumere dei collaboratori, fotografi innanzitutto, alcuni dei quali diventeranno poi, a loro volta, nomi importanti nella storia del fotogiornalismo militare.

Fra essi vi sono: Alexander Gardner, James Gardner, Timothy H. O'Sullivan, William Pywell, George N. Barnard, Thomas C. Roche e tantissimi altri, per un totale di varie decine di persone. A tutti questi fornisce l'attrezzatura da ripresa necessaria e da Washington organizza e coordina le loro attività. Dal suo studio escono copiose le famose immagini che ancora oggi possiamo vedere, conservate in gran parte dalla Libreria del Congresso degli Stati Uniti.

Per la prima volta nella storia delle guerre, delle immagini fotografiche ritraggono dei cadaveri di soldati caduti in battaglia. Ma i soggetti principali sono gli alti ufficiali, sia nordisti che sudisti, primi fra tutti Ulysses Grant e Robert Edward Lee.Soggetti questi, ripresi in vari modi: sotto le tende, vicino a cannoni o in groppa a cavalli.

Viene fotografato in parecchie occasioni dallo stesso Brady anche il presidente dell'Unione Abraham Lincoln: i suoi ritratti sono diventati un classico dell'iconografia di questo grande Presidente. Si stima che in tutta la guerra Brady abbia prodotto non meno di 10.000 stampe.

Egli è considerato di gran lunga il più importante fotoreporter del conflitto e uno dei più grandi fotografi di sempre, oltre che il padre, insieme a Roger Fenton (che illustrò la guerra di Crimea) del fotogiornalismo moderno.

Oltre alle immagini di guerra, Brady fu famoso per la lunga serie di ritratti a personaggi famosi. Dai presidenti americani, agli intellettuali e grandi uomini del tempo come Mark Twain, Edgar Allan Poe, Thomas Edison a personaggi quasi mitici come il generale Custer o Kit Carson, fino al nostro Garibaldi.

Dopo la guerra, una serie di sfortunate circostanze lo ridussero quasi sul lastrico. Stanco e depresso, rimasto vedovo, Brady morì pressoché dimenticato nel 1896, tanto che non si trovarono neppure i soldi per pagarne il funerale, cerimonia di cui si fanno carico i veterani di guerra del 7° Reggimento Fanteria di New York. Il suo corpo riposa oggi a Washington nel cimitero del Congresso.

L'unico limite che ebbero le sue immagini e quelle dei suoi colleghi del tempo, era imposto dalla tecnica allora disponibile,che non permetteva di fare foto di persone o cose in movimento,dato che quelle pionieristiche macchine richiedevano che il soggetto stesse fermo ed immobile per evitare pesanti sfocature.

TIMOTHY O'SULLIVAN (1840-1882)

O'Sullivan nasce nel 1840 in Irlanda. La sua famiglia emigra presto negli Stati Uniti e si stabilisce a New York. A diciotto anni Timothy inizia a lavorare come apprendista presso lo studio di Matthew Brady, fotografo già affermato, con il quale condivide le origini irlandesi. O'Sullivan è fra i primi collaboratori inviati al fronte dallo stesso Brady per documentare fotograficamente lo svolgimento del conflitto. Dimostra subito di essere un valente fotografo, soprattutto per la sua abilità nello sfruttare al meglio le caratteristiche delle fotocamere dell'epoca, certamente poco adatte alla foto di azione; si concentra quindi soprattutto sulle immagini statiche dei campi di battaglia riprese immediatamente dopo la cessazione dei combattimenti, cogliendo scene di grande drammaticità soprattutto per quanto riguarda i particolari dei caduti. Con lui, in coppia, lavora anche Alexander Gardner un, un altro dei fotografi storici della guerra civile americana. Nel 1863 O'Sullivan si separa da Brady e prosegue le riprese di guerra proprio in collaborazione con Gardner, facendo così concorrenza al loro vecchio datore di lavoro. Nel famoso Gardner's Photographic Sketch Book of the War, la prima raccolta di 100 immagini della guerra, sono comprese anche quarantaquattro foto riprese da O'Sullivan.Dopo la guerra ottiene importanti commesse in ambito scientifico e geografico. Dal 1867 al 1869 è il fotografo ufficiale della spedizione scientifica denominata: "United States Geological Exploration of the 40th Parallel", durante la quale fotografa le miniere di Comstock Lode utilizzando l'illuminazione artificiale al magnesio, tecnica rivoluzionaria per l'epoca in quanto sperimentata da pochissimo tempo. Nel 1870 lavora al reportage per la costruzione del canale di Panama. Nel 1871 partecipa ad una spedizione geografica che comporta la documentazione del paesaggio americano e riprende in quella occasione anche splendide immagini presso alcuni indiani pellerossa delle tribù Navajos e Ute. Altri soggetti fanno riferimento alla Central Pacific Railway. O'Sullivan fotografa canyons, laghi e montagne d'America con perizia e arte che lo portano ad essere nominato responsabile del settore fotografico del Ministero del Tesoro statunitense. Malato di tubercolosi muore appena quarantaduenne a New York il 14 gennaio 1882.

▲ **Arlington, Virginia (vicinity).** Gen. Samuel P. Heintzelman and staff at Arlington house. (Mathew B. Brady, the photographer is shown in a top hat in the middle of images)

Arlington, Virginia lo staff Del generale P. Heintzelman ad Arlington house. Mathew B. Brady è presente nella foto con indosso un alto cappello a tuba.

ALEXANDER GARDNER (1821 - 1882)

Curiosamente, dopo gli Irlandesi Brady (almeno di origine) e O'Sullivan, anche il terzo grande fotografo della guerra civile non nasce americano. Gardner infatti nacque in Scozia e si trasferì trentacinquenne negli Stati Uniti nel1856, con lo scopo di sviluppare la sua professione di fotografo. A New York entra in contatto con Brady e ne diviene presto uno dei principali collaboratori. La sua contemporanea amicizia con Allan Pinkerton (che era a capo di un servizio di intelligence che sarebbe poi diventato il servizio segreto americano) gli apre ulteriori possibilità di lavoro. Come per gli altri due citati, anche Gardner deve la sua fama principale alle fotografie riprese durante la guerra civile americana, ma egli fu assai conosciuto anche per le varie riprese al presidente americano Abraham Lincoln, oltre alle immagini dell'esecuzione dei congiurati per l'assassinio dello stesso presidente. Grazie a tutte queste conoscenze, Gardner diventa il fotografo personale del generale George B. Mc Clellan, comandante in capo dell'esercito del Potomac. A questo punto, il fotografo scozzese si ritiene

◄ **The US President Abraham Lincoln** in one of the famous shot of M.Brady.

Il Presidente dell'Unione Abraham Lincoln in un famoso scatto di M.Brady

ormai maturo per mettersi in proprio. Di conseguenza si separa da Brady aprendo, insieme al fratello James un suo studio a Washington, seguito fra l'altro da molti ex dipendenti di Brady.

Nel frattempo Gardner aumenta la sua celebrità fotografando le celebri battaglie di Antietam (1862) di Gettysburg (luglio 1863) e l'assedio di Petersburg (giugno 1864-aprile 1865).

A fine guerra, nel 1866 pubblica un famoso libro fotografico sulla guerra civile (il Gardner's photographic sketch book of the war) composto da circa 100 scatti scelti fra le migliori foto della guerra. Le immagini pubblicate non sono solo sue, ma sono spesso opera di svariati fotografi del suo studio: T. O'Sullivan, James F. Gibson, John Reekie, William Pywell, James Gardner (suo fratello), John Wood, George N. Barnard, David Knox e David Woodbury,

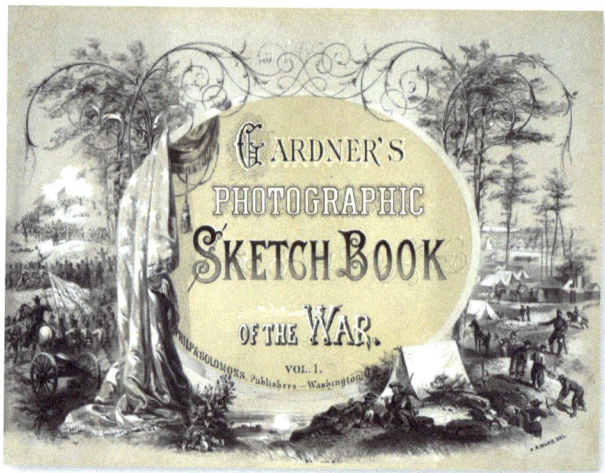

tra gli altri. Dopo la guerra, come già per O'Sullivan, Gardner riceve l'incarico di fotografare i nativi americani che sono venuti a Washington per discutere i trattati di pace. Vivrà a Washington fino alla sua morte avvenuta nel 1882.

▲ **The famous Gardner** photographic Sketchbook of the War cover of 1st volume.

Il famoso Gardner photographic Sketchbook of the War, copertina Del primo volume.

Lo scandalo della messa in scena creata

Nel 1961 alcuni studiosi, elaborando il vasto lavoro fotografico di Gardner, si accorsero che il famoso fotografo, almeno in un'occasione, aveva per così dire montato la "scena". Il giornalista Frederic Ray si accorse infatti che un cadavere di un soldato sudista caduto a Gettysburg e il suo fucile appaiono in due foto diverse. Cosa era accaduto ? Semplicemente era successo che Gardner, aiutato dai suoi assistenti Timothy O'Sullivan e James Gibson, aveva trascinato il corpo di un cecchino sudista 40 metri lontano dal punto esatto dove lo stesso aveva trovato la morte e riposto in una scena più fotogenica nei pressi del famoso e suggestivo Devil's Den. Era questa una prassi ritenuta assai scandalosa nei primi anni della fotografia, e per certi versi discutibile anche oggi.

▼ **The photographic van** of William Redish Pywell in an image of Gardner.

Il carro con le atrezzature fotografiche di William Redish Pywell, qui ripreso dal suo collega Gardner

WILLIAM R. PYWELL(1843 - 1887)

Fotografo americano, Pywell come molti altri, inizia la gavetta con Matthew Brady prima e Alexander Gardner poi. Con quest'ultimo collabora al famoso libro pubblicato da Gardner nel 1866:"Photographic sketch book of the war". Dopo la guerra, esegue riprese fotografiche a carattere geografico -esploratore viaggiando con George Custer come fotografo ufficiale nella Yellowstone Expedition del 1873.

JAMES F. GIBSON (1825-1905)

Gibson nacque a New York City. Nella sua città conosce e lavora per lo studio di Brady. Sono assai note le sue riprese fatte al generale Mc Clellan durante la Campagna Peninsulare, la battaglia dei sette giorni, quella di Gaines'Mille poi di MalvernHill.Morìnel1905.

THOMAS C. ROCHE(1826-1895)

Fotografo al seguito dell'armata del James. A proposito di Roche si racconta un curioso aneddoto che ne esalta il coraggio. Un giorno, mentre sta fotografando nel bel mezzo di una battaglia, un colpo di proiettile d'artiglieria gli esplode vicino. Fortunatamente non lo ferisce, ma in compenso lo riempie di polvere; subito dopo scossa la polvere di dosso, Roche piantò l'apparecchio fotografico nel bel mezzo del cratere causato dalla recente esplosione e riprese a fotografare come se niente fosse.

GEORGE S. COOK (1819-1902)

Il fotografo più noto di parte confederata è stato George Cook. Nato a Stamford in Connecticut nel 1819. Si trasferisce in un primo tempo a New Orleans dove studia arte e diventa un pittore professionista. Nel 1842 scopre la fotografia e si appassiona con il dagherrotipo arrivato in America solo da pochissimi anni. Più tardi, messa su famiglia si sposta con essa a Charleston, South Carolina dove ha modo di entrare in contatto con la realtà della guerra (che inizia proprio in quella città). Un ultimo e definitivo trasferimento lo porta nella capitale sudista Richmond, Virginia, dove realizzerà la più nota e completa raccolta di fotografie di quella città. Morì il 27 novembre 1902.
Celebri le sue immagini di Fort Sumter. Purtroppo però, la maggior parte delle fotografie di Cook sono andate perse in un incendio nel 1864. Cook fra le altre cose fu anche definito il Brady del sud.

ITALIA E USA 150 ANNI DI STORIA

Il 1861è una data che storicamente unisce l'Italia e gli USA. Entrambe condividono un cento cinquantenario. Tuttavia, nel caso italiano, esso delinea la nascita di una nazione. Nel secondo caso il 1861 è invece l'inizio di un pesante conflitto che durerà quattro lunghi anni, e che rischiò di far invece "morire" la giovane nazione dall'altra parte dell'oceano. Per i tanti italiani d'America si trattò quindi di due 150esimi. Sul fronte americano gli italiani di origine o volontari furono presenti e distribuiti in diverse migliaia in entrambe le armate americane. Ricordiamo su tutti i bersaglieri delle "Garibaldi Guard", un reggimento Newyorkese, in cui militarono per l'appunto molti nostri connazionali.

LA GUERRA CIVILE

Attorno al 1850 gli Stati Uniti erano una nazione in forte espansione, impegnati nella conquista degli sconfinati territori del West, che li aveva portati in pochi anni a raggiungere la lontana costa del Pacifico. Impadronitisi con facili guerre, negli anni quaranta, dei territori controllati dal Messico (California,Nuovo Messico, Arizona e Texas) e costrette in piccole riserve le autoctone tribù indiane, antiche popolazioni del continente nordamericano, gli Usa divennero in breve tempo un'enorme nazione,con grandi risorse e potenzialità,ma anche con grandi contrasti al suo interno e con una struttura statale e istituzionale ancora fragile che finì con portare allo scontro militare. Con l'elezione nel 1860 del presidente repubblicano Abramo Lincoln, uno dei più fermi oppositori dello schiavismo e uno degli uomini più legati agli industriali del nord, la frattura fra due mondi e due modi di vedere e pensare alla politica e all'economia americana divenne insanabile.
La Guerra Civile americana, o guerra di Secessione, costituisce ancora oggi l'argomento fondamentale per la storiografia statunitense, non solo perché l'evento costituì il momento più gravido di conseguenze nella storia nazionale nord americana, ma anche perché nelle sue interpretazioni si confrontano idee e analisi spesso in contrasto fra loro e mai del tutto definite. Alla guerra civile appartengono infatti i grandi temi dell'intera storia degli Stati Uniti: da quello del rapporto fra stati e governo federale a quello dello sviluppo economico, da quello della industrializzazione a quello della schiavitù. Argomenti costantemente allo studio di storici, politici, militari ma non solo.
E' tradizione affidare alla questione dello schiavismo la causa scatenante della guerra. Con la contrapposizione fra l'abolizionismo voluto da Lincoln, il grande presidente della guerra, e le necessità commerciali e non solo dell'aristocratica classe dirigente sudista. Uno dei massimi analisti della storia del conflitto fu James Ford Rhodes che con il suo History of the Civil War, per primo associò al problema pur portante dello schiavismo, l'ipotesi di un antagonismo complesso fra le due parti contrapposte in termini economici, politici e sociali. Anche perché già al tempo vi era comunque la netta percezione, che anche al sud il fenomeno arcaico e reazionario, per quanto ampiamente integrato nel tessuto sociale dello schiavismo, fosse finalmente e spontaneamente destinato a concludersi nel corso di qualche anno o decennio. Se questa tesi fosse destinata, come pare, a fare breccia nella storiografia ufficiale ne deriverebbe l'ipotesi di un conflitto tutt'altro che inevitabile perché basato su problemi assai più ampi e complessi. Lo schiavismo insomma non dava tutte

le risposte ai numerosi perché. Il conflitto prese piede pertanto per svariate ragioni. Dalle motivazioni classiche di sciovinismo e localismo che preludevano al fanatismo più bieco che divisero fatalmente il sudista Johnny Reb dal nordista Billy Yankee, a complicazioni più squisitamente politiche con la suddivisione anche fisica e geografica del bipartitismo americano: repubblicani al Nord e democratici al Sud. La storia narra quindi che nel febbraio del 1861, undici stati del sud andarono a formare la "Confederazione", una sorta di nazione autonoma. Gli Stati Confederati d'America raggruppavano la Carolina del Sud, il Mississippi, la Florida, l'Alabama, la Georgia, la Louisiana, il Texas, la Virginia, l'Arkansas, il Tennessee e la Carolina del Nord. Il Nord, non accettando questa frattura, decise inevitabilmente l'apertura dello scontro che diede vita a una guerra lunga e sanguinosissima (con 600.000 morti), la più cruenta dai tempi delle campagne napoleoniche. La guerra civile fu anche il primo conflitto moderno grazie al grande apporto dell'industria (specialmente al Nord), all'uso massiccio della ferrovia e allo sviluppo della moderna artiglieria. Durante la guerra ci furono anche invenzioni rivoluzionarie come il sottomarino, le corazzature dei battelli, il diffondersi dei più recenti sistemi di comunicazione come il telegrafo e la stessa fotografia che divennero fondamentali per avere notizie rapide e precise sul nemico. Tutto ciò rese questa guerra un "conflitto totale" che si dimostrò pertanto assai micidiale per i combattenti che infatti lamentarono un numero di vittime mai visto prima in battaglia.

La guerra si concluse con l'annunciata (ed inevitabile) vittoria degli stati del Nord, economicamente più forti. La sconfitta del Sud portò alla fine immediata dello schiavismo, che per la sua repentina attuazione fu un colpo micidiale per le economie sostanzialmente agricole degli stati ex confederati. La guerra civile americana finì comunque con l'accelerare un'impressionante esplosione industriale. Le ferrovie collegarono le due coste, gli indiani subirono le ultime pesanti sconfitte e vennero definitivamente soffocate le loro giuste aspirazioni. Gli Usa, nel giro di pochi decenni dopo Appomatox, l'amena località dove Lee firmò nelle mani di Ulisse Grant la resa definitiva del Sud, sarebbero diventati una delle più grandi potenze mondiali.

▲ Lt. Col. A. Ripetti, 39th N.Y. Inf.
Most of the Italians who joined the Union Army were recruited from New York City. The Garibaldi Guard was the name of the 39th New York Infantry. His commander was the Col. Frederick George D'Utassy. Between 5,000 and 10,000 Italians fought in the Civil War for both the Union and the Confederacy. Four were Union generals, including General Luigi Palma di Cesnola, who was wounded, and who received the Medal of Honor and was later the first director of New York's Metropolitan Museum of Art. The coat for the officers of "Garibaldi Guard" was dark blue with gold frogging on the bast and gold lace on the sleeves. The men had red trim on their coats and "bersaglieri" hat.

Tenente Colonello A. Ripetti, del 39° N.Y. Inf.
Gli italiani parteciparono numerosi alla Guerra Civile americana in entrambi gli schieramenti. Si calcola che circa 11.000 americani avevano dichiarato di essere nati in Italia. Il più noto di questi reggimenti fu il "Garibaldi Guards" o 39° New York Infantry Regiment che usava la bandiera italiana usata nel 1848 da Garibaldi in Lombardia e nel 1849 a Roma. I soldati del reggimento indossavano come parte dell'uniforme, il cappello dei Bersaglieri, la tunica blu scuro con filettature rosse (oro per gli ufficiali). Le Garibaldi Guard rimasero in servizio dal 28 maggio 1861 al 1 luglio 1865. Il reggimento fu arruolato il 27 maggio 1861 a New York sotto il comando del colonnello Frederick George D'Utassy.

THE CIVIL WAR PHOTOS

GLI UOMINI CHE FECERO LA GUERRA CIVILE AMERICANA - LE FOTO

Billy Yankee, the Union soldier

Billy Yankee, il soldato nordista

◄ **Col. George L. Willard, 125th N.Y. Inf.**
George Lamb Willard was born in New York
the August 15, 1827 and died at Gettysburg the
July 2, 1863. He was an officer in the Union
Army who commanded a New York regiment
and, briefly, a brigade in the American Civil
War. He lost his life leading the brigade in
the II Corps at the Battle of Gettysburg.
Before he had served in the Mexican War.
As many militiamen, Willard like the French
uniform style. In this image observe the gray-
blue overcoat lined and trimmed on his left
shoulder.

***Colonnello George L. Willard, 125th N.Y.
Infantry.***
*George Lamb Willard nacque a new York nel
1827. Dopo aver combattuto nella Guerra
messicana fa una rapida carriera che lo porta
a comandare il 125 reggimento di New York,
e per breve tempo anche una brigata. Trovo
la morte alla guida del suo reggimento, il due
luglio del 1863 a Gettysburg. Come molto
ufficiali americani del periodo, Willard amava
lo stile militare francese. Nell'immagine
vediamo il tipico cappotto grigio-azzurro con
gli alamari alla francese posto sulla spalla
sinistra.*

◄ **May 20, 1862 Virginia. The staff of Gen. Fitz-John Porter;
Lts. William G. Jones and George A. Custer reclining.**
Photographs from the main Eastern theater of War: the Peninsular
Campaign, May-August 1862. A shot by James F. Gibson. This
image documents that the staff of a General had it much better
than the typical soldier. These officers can be seen enjoying what
appears to be wine and other fine spirits. It is interesting to note
that Custer is pictured with a dog. He appears to be a dog lover,
because he is often pictured with a dog nearby.

20 maggio 1862, Virginia. Il Gen. Fitz-John Porter e il suo staff.
*I due personaggi distesi sono il tenente G. Jones William e
George A. Custer. Foto scattata da F.Gibson nella campagna
della penisola. Questo documento sembra mostrare la migliore
situazione generale degli ufficiali rispetto ai soldati. E 'interessante
notare che Custer è qui raffigurato con un cane. Dato che egli
è spesso raffigurato con un cane vicino, possiamo desumere che
fosse un amante di questi animali.*

► **An Union officer of infantry in full dress coat.** Unknown
photograph, date and location.

Un ufficiale di fanteria nordista in alta uniforme. Fotografo, data
e località sconosciute.

▲ **May 1862. "Yorktown, Virginia (vicinity). Group before the photographic tent at Camp Winfield Scott."** From photographs of the Peninsular Campaign, May-August 1862. An image shot by James F. Gibson.

Maggio 1862 "Yorktown, Virginia, Gruppo davanti alla tenda nel campo trincerato di Winfield Scott." Dalle foto della campagna della penisola 1862. Foto di J. F. Gibson.

◄ **Bealeton, Va. Co. D, 93d New York Infantry.** In a Union army camp, these six non commissioned officers relax and share a bite to eat together.

Bealeton, Virginia Comp. D, 93° New York Infantry. In una tenda da campo nordista questi sei sottufficiali si rilassano e bevono insieme su uno stretto tavolo.

24

► **7th N.Y. State Militia officer** posed in full uniform holding drawn sword. Camp Cameron, D.C. 1861

7° N.Y. State Militia, Ufficiale in alta uniforme in classica posa con sciabola sguainata a Camp Cameron D.C nel 1861.

▼ **Col. James E. McMahon, 164th New York Infantry** in a shot of M.Brady

Col. James E. McMahon, 164° New York Infantry in una foto di M.Brady

▼ **(at right) Col. N.B. Hyde, 37th Vermont Infantry** This infantry officer posed for the portrait in about 1864. He is wearing the official dark blue jachet and trousers. Note the eagle on the shoulder straps to indicate his grade of Colonel.

(a destra) Colonnello N.B. Hyde, comandante del 37th Vermont Infantry.
Il colonnello è in posa per l'usuale ritratto attrono al 1864. Egli indossa la tipica tenuta d'ordinanza blu scuro a doppio petto. Notate l'aquila sulle spalline a denotare il suo grado di colonnello.

▲ Maj. H. W. Sawyer and staff at Camp Stoneman District of Columbia
A classical tent photo for this US cavalry regiment staff. His commander , the Major Sawyer stands seated in the centre surrounded by his officers photographed in more tranquil times early in the War.

Il maggiore H.W.Sawyer ed il suo staff a Camp Stoneman nel distretto di Columbia
Una classica foto sotto la tenda da campo per lo stato maggiore di questo reggimento di cavalleria. Il comandante, maggiore Sawyer è seduto nel mezzo circondato dai suoi ufficiali ripresi nella calma degli ultimi giorni di Guerra.

▶ Lt. E.K. Butler, 69th N.Y.S.M.
An officer in full dress coat of 69th New York State Militia. This Regiment is a military unit from New York City, part of the New York Army National Guard. It is known as the Fighting (Irish) Sixty-Ninth, a name said to have been given to it by Robert E. Lee during the Civil War.

Tenente E.K.Butler del 69° N.Y.S.M.
Un ufficiale in alta uniforme del 69° New York State Militia. Questo reggimento er un unità che proveniva dalla Guardia nazionale di New York. Conosciuto anche con il nome di Fighting Irish (lottatori Irlandesi) Sixty-Ninth, a nome che si disse venne loro affibbiato dal comandante sudista R.E.Lee.

▲ **Six Unionist General officer. Hugh Judson Kilpatrick (1836-1881)** known as "Kill-cavalry" for using tactics in battle that were considered as a reckless disregard for lives of soldiers under his command, Kilpatrick was both praised for the victories he achieved, and despised by southerners whose homes and towns he devastated. **Ulysses S. Grant (1822-1885)** military commander of Union Army and later the 18th President of the United States (1869–1877). Under Grant's command, the Union Army defeated the Confederate military and ended the Confederate States of America. **Joshua Lawrence Chamberlain (1828-1914)** was an American college professor from the State of Maine. For his gallantry at Gettysburg, he was awarded the Medal of Honor. He was given the honor of commanding the Union troops at the surrender ceremony for the infantry of Robert E. Lee's Army at Appomattox, Virginia. **General A. B. Underwood** start his military career us captain of 2nd regiment of the Massachusetts Volunteer Militia and later promoted to general. **James Barnet Fry (1827–1894)** was an American soldier and prolific author of historical books. **Louis Douglas Watkins (1833-1868)** he was severely wounded at Gaines's Mills he engaged in several campaign on western front of the war: Nashville, Chickamauga, Chattanooga and Atlanta.

Sei generali superiori dell'armata nordista. Hugh Judson Kilpatrick (1836-1881) soprannominato "Kill-cavalry" per la sua ardita tattica di combattimento pericolosa per i suoi uomini, Kilpatrick venne anche stigmatizzato per le distruzioni fatte alle città del Sud da lui conquistate. Ulysses S. Grant (1822-1885) comandante in capo dell'armata nordista e futuro 18° Presidente degli Stati Uniti (1869–1877). Sotto il suo comando il Nord sconfisse gli stati confederati in maniera definitiva. Joshua Lawrence Chamberlain (1828-1914) professore americano del college dello stato del Maine. Per la sua galanteria a Gettysburg, gli venne concessa la Medaglia d'Onore. Gli fu anche concesso l'onore di comandare le truppe nordiste alla cerimonia della resa di Lee ad Appomattox in Virginia. Generale A. B. Underwood iniziò la sua carriera come capitano del 2° reggimento del Massachusetts Volunteer Militia e più tardi promosso generale. James Barnet Fry (1827–1894) oltre alla carriera militare egli fu un prolifico autore di libri di storia. Louis Douglas Watkins (1833-1868) seriamente ferito a Gaines's Mills , fu presente in numerose campagna sul fronte ovest della guerra: Nashville, Chickamauga, Chattanooga e Atlanta.

▲ **Scene showing deserted camp and wounded soldier (zouave)** Various militia units in both the armies of Civil War adaptded the zouave dress style in many ways from the French uniformology tradition. In this fine shot of M.Brady we see a wounded union zouave in the traditional short racket with lace and large red trousers.

Un soldato rifocilla uno zuavo ferito sul campo. Molte unità di miliziani di entrambe le armate impegnate nella Guerra Civile adottarono la tenuta alla zuava di antica tradizione uniformologica francese (a sua volta adottata in Africa attorno al 1830). In questa bella immagine di M.Brady vediamo uno zuavo ferito che indossa la tipica giacchetta con lacci e i tipici larghi pantaloni rossi.

▶ **Photo of an unidentified woman (vivandiere)** of the Union Army during the Civil War who is wearing a kepi and a canteen and a dress in French style.

Cantiniera non identificata dell'esercito nordista. La donna indossa un'uniforme di chiara tradizione francese con chepì e borraccia.

▲ **Six Unionist General officer: Christopher Columbus Andrews (1829-1922)** was an American soldier, diplomat, newspaperman, author, and forester. He participated in the Vicksburg Campaign. **Fitz John Porter (1822-1901)** He is most known for his performance at the Second Battle of Bull Run and his subsequent court martial. Although Porter served well in the early battles of the Civil War, but his military career was ruined by the controversial trial. Afterwards he worked intensely to restore his reputation. **Lorenzo Thomas (1804-1875)** was Adjutant General of the Army at the beginning of the American Civil War. After the war, he was appointed temporary Secretary of War by President Andrew Johnson, precipitating Johnson's impeachment. **Joseph Horace Eaton (1815-1896)** was an American artist painter and Army officer. aide-de-camp and military secretary to Maj. Gen. John C. Frémont   He was promoted to general in 1865. **William Thomas Ward (1808-1878)** was a brigadier general of Kentucky. Ward led a brigade in XX Corps during the early stages of the Atlanta Campaign. He also led it in Sherman's March to the Sea and the Carolinas Campaign. **Montgomery Cunningham Meigs (1816-1892)** was a career United States Army officer, civil engineer, construction engineer for a number of facilities in Washington, D.C., and Quartermaster General of the U.S. Army during and after the American Civil War.

Sei generali superiori dell'armata nordista: Christopher Columbus Andrews (1829-1922) soldato, giornalista, scrittore, diplomatico e agronomo. Partecipò alla campagna di Vicksburg. Fitz John Porter (1822-1901) noto per l'episodio della seconda Bull Run che lo portò alla Corte Marziale. Successivamente Porter servì egregiamente per il resto della guerra ma la sua carriera militare venne comunque scossa e gli ci vollero ben 25 anni per restaurare la sua reputazione. Lorenzo Thomas (1804-1875) aiutante di campo generale durante la guerra, dopo la guerra fu brevemente segretario della difesa del Presidente Andrew Johnson. Joseph Horace Eaton (1815-1896) soldato e pittore di fama americano. Aiutante di campo del Gen. John C. Frémont. Venne promosso generale nel 1865. William Thomas Ward (1808-1878) Militare del Kentucky. Ward guidò una brigata durante la campagna di Atlanta. Più tardi seguì Sherman nella cosiddetta "Marcia al mare". Montgomery Cunningham Meigs (1816-1892) Soldato di carriera, ingegnere civile e delle costruzioni, Quartermaster General dell'armata nordista durante la Guerra Civile.

◄ A Union Volunteer of 7th N.Y. National Guard
Despite the popular preference for the dark blue in the Northern army, some union regiments started the War in gray, such as the 7th New York State Militia. The uniform was all in light grey with black trimming. The kepi bore the company number in brass metal. On the brass waist belt and on cartridge pouch plare appear the initials "N.G.". The regiment was armed with the 1855 rifle musket.

Volontario nordista del 7° N.Y. National Guard
In dispetto del tradizionale amore per il blu scuro, simbolo delle armate nordiste, qualche reggimento unionista iniziò la Guerra in grigio come il caso di questo 7° New York State Militia. L'uniforme completamente grigio chiaro era filettata in nero. Il chepì portava il numero della compagnia in bronzo. La placca in bronzo del cinturone e quella posta sulla giberna recava le cifre "N.G." (Guardia Nazionale). Il reggimento era armato con il moschetto mod. 1855.

▼ ▼ ▼ Other men of 7th New York State Militia.
from left to right: the sergeants Cozzens, Oscar Ryder and James J.Morrison

Altri uomini del 7° New York State Militia.
Da sinistra a destra i sergenti: Cozzens, Oscar Ryder e James J.Morrison

▲ Manassas, Va. Men of Co. C, 41st New York Infantry. Shot of Timothy H. O'Sullivan. Photograph from the main eastern theater of the war, Bull Run, 2nd Battle of, Va., 1862, July-August 1862.

Manassas, Virginia. Uomini della compagnia C, del 41° New York Infantry. Immagine di Timothy H. O'Sullivan. Foto dal fronte principale ad Est , seconda battaglia di Bull Run, luglio-agosto 1862.

► Capt. Schwartz, sharpshooter, 39th New York Regiment. (Garibaldi Guard).

Curiosa immagine Del capitano Schwartz, del 39° reggimento sharpshooter, New York. (Garibaldi Guard).

◄ **Unidentified African American Union soldier 1863/1865** A study shot of the photographer Enoch Long (1823-1898) of an African American Union soldier with a rifle and revolver in front of painted backdrop showing weapons and American flag at Benton Barracks, Saint Louis, Missouri.

Ritratto di un soldato di colore dell'armata nordista non identificato 1863-1865Foto da studio del fotografo Enoch Long (1823-1898) che mostra il soldato americano in posa con fucile e pistola sullo sfondo dipinto con allegorie militari delle caserme di Benton a Saint Louis nel Missouri.

► **Pvt. Francis E. Brownell of the 11th NY Fire Zouaves** The zouave Brownell on May 23rd, 1861, accompanied his colonel Elmer Ellsworth into Alexandria's Marshall House hotel to pull down a secession banner flying from the building and visible though a glass from the White House. As Ellsworth descended the stairs with the flag he was killed by a shotgun blast fired by the hotel's proprietor, James Jackson. Brownell, who was with Ellsworth, quickly shot Jackson in the face, then drove his saber bayonet through his body. Ellsworth became a dead hero in the North, mourned by his friend Abraham Lincoln. Jackson received similar posthumous honors in the south. Brownell became a living celebrity, whose photo, complete with Ellsworth's blood stained banner, became a popular item.

Il soldato Francis E.Brownell del 11° N.Y. (Fire) zuavi Lo zuavo Brownell, il 23 maggio 1861 accompagnò il suo colonnello Elmer Ellsworth presso l'Alexandria Marshall House Hotel da dove sventolava una bandiera secessionista visibile persino dalla casa bianca. Mentre il colonnello Ellsworth discendeva le scale con la bandiera rimossa venne affrontato dal proprietario dell'hotel, tale James Jackson che lo uccise con una fucilata. Browell si gettò subito sull'assassino uccidendolo a sua volta con la baionetta del suo fucile. Ellsworth divenne uno dei primi eroi morti nel Nord, compianto dal suo amico Abraham Lincoln. Il "confederato" Jackson ricevette analoghi riconoscimenti postumi, nel sud. Brownell divenne invece una celebrità vivente, la cui foto, completa della bandiera macchiata di sangue Ellsworth posta ai suoi piedi divenne un famoso elemento popolare.

► **Five soldiers, four unidentified, in Union uniforms** of the 6th Regiment Massachusetts Volunteer Militia outfitted with Enfield muskets in front of encampment. The identified soldier is Albert L. Burgess, on far right.

Cinque soldati du cui 4 non identificati del 6° reggimento Massachusetts Volunteer Militia armati con moschetto Enfield in posa di fronte al proprio accampamento. Il soldato noto si chiama Albert L.Burgess (all'estrema destra).

▲ **Generals Sheridan (at right), Kautz (seated), and friend.** Philip Henry Sheridan (1831-1888) was one of the most famous federal general of the war. August Valentine Kautz (1828 – 1895) was a German-American soldier and Union Army cavalry.

I generali Sheridan (a destra), Kautz (seduto), e un amico. Philip Henry Sheridan (1831-1888) fu uno dei più famosi generali federali della guerra. August Valentine Kautz (1828 – 1895) generale di cavalleria di origini tedesche.

► **Lieutenant Colonel R. Peard 9th Massachusetts infantry**

Il tenente colonnello R. Peard del 9° reggimento di fanteria del Massachusetts.

▲ **Bealeton, Virginia. Capt. Henry Page, assistant quarter master, at Army of the Potomac Headquarters**
The Captain Page was born in New Castle, Delaware, and was a son of Captain John Page, who was killed in the battle of Palo Alo in the Mexican War. He enlisted in the Chicago Light Artillery when the Civil War began. He rose through the various grades until he was a Captain when the War ended. Page served with the Army of thePotomac and took part in the battles of Yorktown, Richmond, Gaines's Mill, White Oak Swamp, Malvern Hill, Second Bull Run, Antietam, Gettysburg and a number of others. (in the small image another photo of the same officer).

Il capitano Henry Page, attendente al quartier generale dell'armata del Potomac
Il capitano Page nacque a New Castle nel Delaware. Figlio del capitano J.Page che morì nella battaglia di palo Alto nella Guerra contro il Mexico. Inizia la Guerra Civile arruolandosi nell'artiglieria leggera di Chicago, divenne capitano verso la fine della Guerra. Pages servì con onore nell'armata del Potomac e prese parte a numerose battaglie fra le quali: Yorktown, Richmond, Gaines's Mill, White Oak Swamp, Malvern Hill, Second Bull Run, Antietam, Gettysburg. (nell'immagine piccola un'altra foto dello stesso ufficiale).

► **A Group of officers near the tent of 16th Pennsylvania Volunteers Cavalry.** The troops comprising this regiment were recruited in the city of Philadelphia, and in several nearest counties.

Un gruppo di ufficiali del 16° Pennsylvania Volunteers Cavalry vicino alla tenda da campo. Le truppe di questo reggimento vennero arruolate nella città di Filadelfia, e delle contee vicine.

▼ **Lt. Col. J.H. Childs, 4th Pa. Cavalry** in two different shot.

Il tenete colonnello J.H.Childs del 4° Pennsylvania cavalry in due differenti pose.

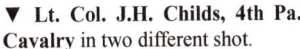

◀ **Lt. Col. Wm. B. Hyde, 9th N.Y. Cavalry** A proud determined pose of the young officer in full dress coat with gauntleted hand resting on massive sabre of the 9th Regiment New York Volunteer Cavalry, also known as the Stoneman Cavalry. This regiment was present at Gettysburg with the 2nd brigade, 1st divison of gen. Buford.The 9th New York claimed that the first shot of the battle was fired by its Corporal Alpheus Hodges. But in a controversy that continues to this day, the claim was challenged by the 8th Illinois Cavalry.The regiment was commanded at Gettysburg by Colonel William Sackett. It brought 395 men to the field, losing two killed, two wounded and seven missing.

Tenente colonnello William B.Hyde del 9° N.Y.Cavalry La fiera immagine di un giovane ufficiale in alta uniforme appartenente al 9° reggimento New York Volunteer Cavalry, noto anche col nome di Stoneman Cavalry (uomini di pietra). Il reggimento fu presente a Gettysburg all'interno della seconda brigata, 1° divisione di cavalleria sotto il comando del generale Buford. Il 9° reclama l'onore del primo sparo della battaglia da parte del suo caporale Alpheus Hodges. Questa convinzione non è però apprezzata dai rappresentanti del 8° Illinois cavalry che reclamano per loro questo fatto. Il reggimento a Gettysburg era al comando del colonnello William Sackett. Composto da 395 uomini, lamentò nella battaglia due morti, due feriti e sette dispersi.

▶ **An Unidentified soldier in Union uniform** with saber and horse with a McClellan saddle and roll behind the saddle labeled 4.

Un soldato di cavalleria non identificato con uniforme nordista, cavallo con la tipica sella detta McClellan con coperta arrotolata recante il numero 4 (del reggimento ?).

▲ Col. Percy Wyndham, 1st N.J. Cavalry

Col. Percy Wyndham, 1° N.J. Cavalry

▲ **Westover Landing, Va. Col. James H. Childs** (standing) with other officers of the 4th Pennsylvania Cavalry. Photograph from the main eastern theater of war, the Peninsular Campaign, May-August 1862. A shot of Alexander Gardner.

Westover Landing, Virhinia. Il Col. James H. Childs (disteso) con altri ufficiali Del 4° Pennsylvania Cavalry. Foto dal fronte Est della guerra. Campagna della penisola, maggio-agosto 1862. Foto di Alexander Gardner.

◄ **Lieut. Colonel A.V. Colburn,** Warrenton, Va., November, 1862 a full-length portrait, on horseback, facing left.

Il tenente colonnello A.V. Colburn, a Warrenton, Virginia nel novembre 1862.

◄ **Gen. George A. Custer, U.S.A. The "Boy General"**
George Armstrong Custer today is most remembered fort he disastrous military engagement known as the Battle of the Little Bighorn. Born in December 1839, Custer raised in Michigan and Ohio, he was admitted to West Point in 1858, where he graduated last in his class. However, with the outbreak of the Civil War, all officers were needed, and Custer was called to serve with the Union Army. Custer acquired a solid reputation during the Civil War, and he became the most younger major general of US army in 1865 at the age of twenty five. Custer was well known in the US army also for his extravagant and curious manner and dress. In this portrait of LC collection, shot by Matthew Brady the 23 may 1865, he wore a dark blue short jacket, with an informal sky blue sailor collar, a red cravat at the neck, blue trousers with double gold strips and black cavalry boots. Under the wide-brimmed hat his characteristic long and blond hair !

Generale A. George Custer, U.S.A. il "Boy General"
George Armstrong Custer, il famoso generale americano notissimo da noi soprattutto per la tragica battaglia del Little Big Horne i cui perse la vita insieme a tutti i suoi uomini (solo un trombettiere di origine italiana, tale Martini, riuscì a farla franca). Nato alla fine del 1839, cresciuto fra Michigan ed Ohio, venne ammesso a West Point nel 1858, dove ebbe il demerito di classificarsi ultimo nella sua classe. Tuttavia, lo scoppio della Guerra Civile, necessitava di ogni uomo valido, e così anche per Custer venne l'ora di servire la patria. Sui campi di battaglia ebbe modo di riscattarsi costruendo una solida reputazione di abile e coraggioso comandante, fino a divenire il più giovane generale dell'armata unionista a soli 25 anni. La sua notorietà gli derivava anche dalla sua stravaganza nei modi di fare e nel vestire.
In questa nota immagine scattata da M.Brady nel maggio del 1865, lo vediamo indossare una corta giacca blu con uno strambo colletto alla marinara color azzurro cielo fuori ordinanza. Una cravatta rossa sgargiante, pantaloni blu con doppia banda e stivali da cavalleria. Sotto il largo capellaccio i suoi epici e lunghi cappelli biondi !

► **Westover Landing, Va. Col. William W. Averell, 3d Pennsylvania Cavalry, and his staff**
In this photo of Alexander Gardner (1821-1882) from the main eastern theater of War, the Peninsular Campaign, May-August 1862. Sitters standing Left to right: Lt. W.H. Brown, 5th U.S. Cavalry; Lt. H.H. King, 3d Pennsylvania Cavalry; Colonel Averell the commander of regiment; Lt. Phillip Pollard, 3rd Pennsylvania Cavalry.
William Woods Averell (1832-1900) was a career United States Army officer and a cavalry general in the American Civil War. After the War he was a diplomat and became wealthy by inventing American asphalt pavement.

Westover Landing (Virginia). Il colonnello W.Averell comandante del 3° Pennsylvania Cavalry con il suo staff.
Foto di Alexander Gardner, con Brady uno dei più noti fotografi della Guerra Civile. Ripresa effettuata nell'agosto del 1862 durante la campagna della penisola. Da sinistra a destra: il tenente W.H. Brown, del 5° U.S. Cavalry; il tenente H.H. King, del 3° Pennsylvania Cavalry; il colonnello Averell (seduto) comandante del reggimento ed infine il tenente Phillip Pollard del 3° Pennsylvania Cavalry.
William Woods Averell (1832–1900) divenne in seguito generale di cavalleria. Dopo la Guerra intraprese la carriere diplomatica ed in seguito divenne ricchissimo grazie al suo brevetto relativo all'invenzione dell'asfalto per pavimentazione.

► Col. A.T. McReynolds, 1st NY Cavalry *Col. A.T. McReynolds, 1° NY Cavalry*

▼ **Staff officers at headquarters, Army of Potomac, April 1863**
From left: Capt. Alexander Moore, Capt. Harry Russell and Capt. W.L. Candler on horseback
Ufficiali di Stato maggiore armata Del Potomac, aprile 1863 *Da sinistra: Cap. Alexander Moore, Cap. Harry Russell e Cap. W.L. Candler.*

► **Six officers of the 17th New York Battery**, probably at Camp Barry, near Washington, D.C. in a shot of David Knox, May 1863.
From left to right: Unidentified man, 1st Lieut. Irving Meade Thompson, 2nd Lieut. Edwin Joel Barber, Capt. George Tobey Anthony, 1st Lieut. Hiram E. Sickels, and 2nd Lieut. Hiram D. Smith. Photograph from the main eastern theater of the war, near the time of the Battle of Gettysburg, June-July 1863. But, the 17th NY Battery did not go to Gettysburg.

Sei ufficiali del 17° New York Battery, probabilmente a Camp Barry, nei pressi di Washington, D.C. in una foto di David Knox, maggio1863.
Da sinistra a destra: personaggio non identificato, tenente Irving Meade Thompson, sottotenente Edwin Joel Barber, Capitano George Tobey Anthony, tenente Hiram E. Sickels, e sottotenente Hiram D. Smith. Foto dal fronte est della guerra al tempo della battaglia di Gettysburg, giugno-luglio 1863. Tuttavia il 17° NY non fu presente alla grande battaglia.

► **Washington, District of Columbia. Officers of 3d Regiment Massachusetts Heavy Artillery** in pose on a giant gun !!

Washington, Distretto di Columbia. Ufficiali del 3° reggimento Massachusetts Heavy Artillery in posa su un cannone gigante !!

▲ **Maj. A.G. Enos, 8th Cavalry**

Maggiore A.G. Enos, 8° Reg. Cavalry

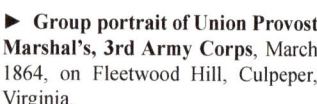

► **Group portrait of Union Provost Marshal's, 3rd Army Corps**, March 1864, on Fleetwood Hill, Culpeper, Virginia.

Gruppo di ufficiali nordisti Della sussistenza Del 3° corpo d'armata, Marzo 1864, a Fleetwood Hill, Culpeper, Virginia.

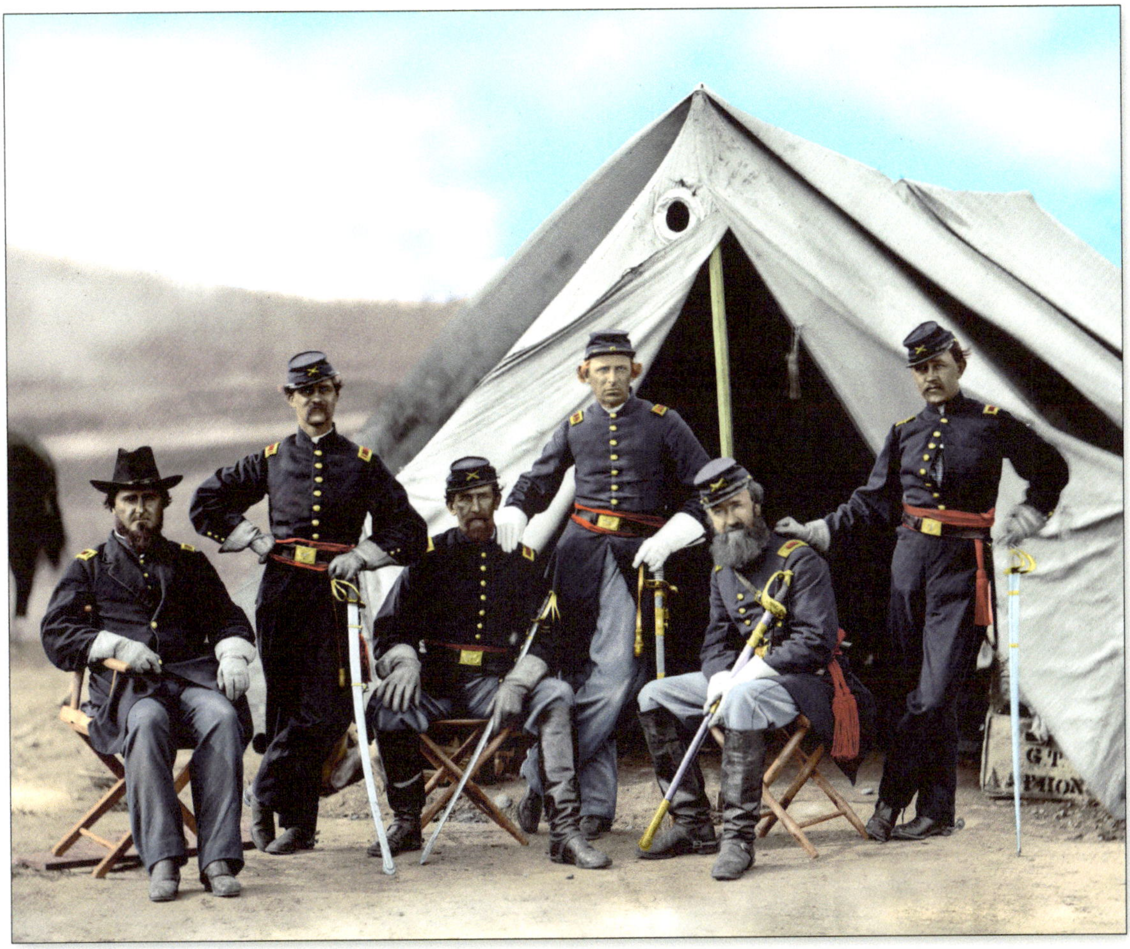

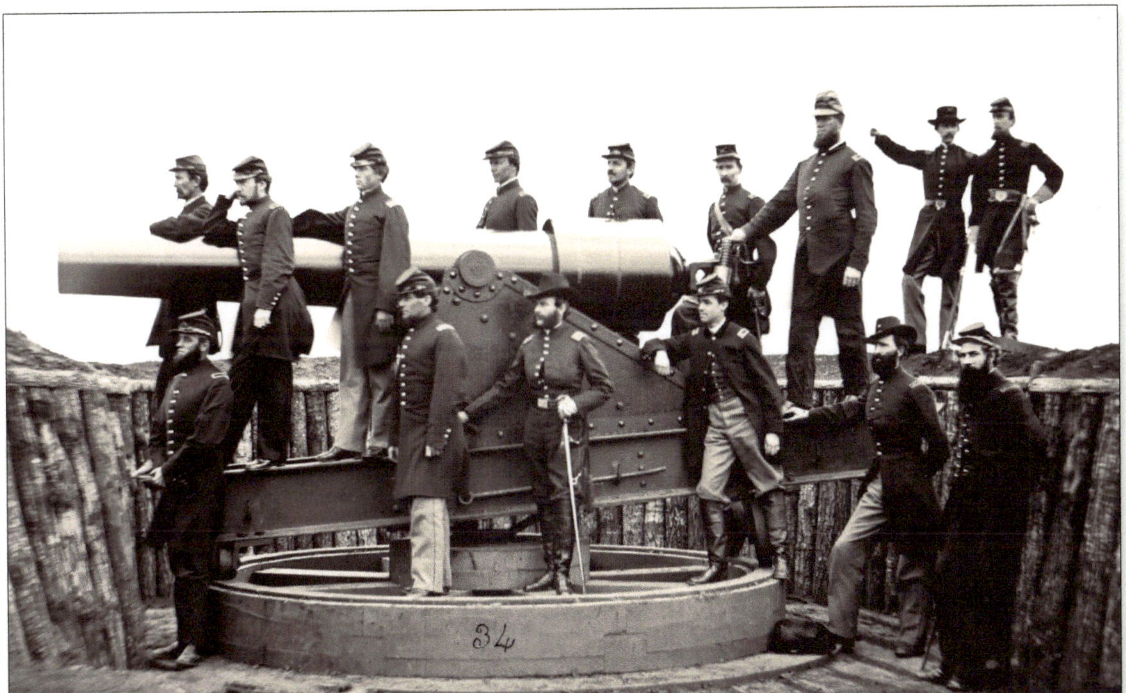
34

▲ **Fair Oaks, Va., vicinity. Officers of Battery A, 2nd U.S. Artillery. R. Clarke, Tidball, Dennison and Pennington. June 1862**
A photo by James F. Gibson from the main eastern theater of War, the Peninsular Campaign, May-August 1862. The Battery A, 2nd U.S. Artillery (2nd Regiment of Artillery) with his commander, the Captain John C. Tidball, USA, of Ohio (the second from left, and his staff: Lt. Robert Clarke (left), Lt. William N. Dennison (at right of Tidball), and Capt. Alexander C.M. Pennington at estreme right. Originally under the direct command of Lt. Col. (and future Brigadier General) William Hays, and later under the two-brigade command of captains James Madison Robertson and John C. Tidball, the Horse Artillery served with distinction during most of the major engagements in the Eastern Theater.

Fair Oaks, Virginia. Ufficiali della Batteria A, 2° U.S. Artillery. R. Clarke, Tidball, Dennison e Pennington. Giugno 1862.
Famosa foto di James Gibson ripresa durante la campagna della penisola del maggio-agosto 1862 che ritrae lo staff della batteria A del 2° US Artillery. Da sinistra a destra: il tenente Robert Clarke, il capitano e comandante della batteria John C. Tidball , il tenente William N. Dennison ed il capitano Alexander C.M. Pennington. Originariamente sotto il comando del colonnello e poi generale William Hays e più tardi sotto il diretto comando dei due capitani James Madison Robertson e John C. Tidball, l'artiglieria a cavallo unionista servì con distinzione in tutti i maggior teatri dell'est.

▶ **Fair Oaks, Va., vicinity. Capt. Rufus D. Pettit's Battery B, 1st New York Light Artillery, in Fort Richardson.** Photograph from the main eastern theater of war, the Peninsular Campaign, May-August 1862 by George N. Barnard (1819-1902).

Fair Oaks, Virginia. La Pettit's Battery B, 1st New York Light Artillery, del capitano D.Rufus a Fort Richardson. Foto dal fronte orientale della guerra, (Peninsular Campaign), maggio-agosto 1862 scattata da George N. Barnard (1819-1902).

◄ **Washington, District of Columbia. Officers and men, 3d Regiment Massachusetts Heavy Artillery in Fort Totten.** Construction of Fort Totten began in August 1861 and was finished by 1863. It occupied a high point in advance of the Soldiers' Home, President's Lincoln summer home. It mounted 20 guns and mortars, including eight 32-pounders. The fort's 100-pounder Parrott rifle provided long-range support to Fort Stevens during Confederate General Jubal A. Early's attack on that fort on July 11 and 12, 1864.

Washington, distretto di Columbia. Uomini e ufficiali del 3° reggimento di artiglieria pesante del Massachusetts a Fort Totten. La costruzione di Fort Totten ebbe inizio nel mese di agosto 1861 e fu terminata nel 1863. Esso occupava una posizione strategica elevata nei pressi della tenuta estiva del Presidente Lincoln. Armato con fra 20 cannoni e mortai, di cui otto da 32 libbre.

▲ **Fair Oaks, Va., vicinity. Capt. Horatio G. Gibson** (second from left) and officers of his battery. Photo of James F. Gibson in 1862 June.

Fair Oaks, Virginia. Il capitano Horatio G. Gibson (secondo da sinistra) con gli ufficiali della sua batteria. Foto di James F. Gibson del giugno 1862.

▲ **Officers and men of Keystone Battery** 1863 From a photo of M. Mathew Brady.

Uomini e ufficiali della batteria Keystone . foto del 1863 di M.Brady.

▲ **Washington, District of Columbia. Wiard gun at U.S. Arsenal.** From a photo of M. Mathew Brady.

Washington, Distretto di Columbia. Cannone modello Wiard presso l'arsenale centrale. Da una foto di Mathew Brady.

▲ **Battery No. 4 near Yorktown 13 inch mortar** The Battery No. 4 mounting 10 13-inch mortars, each weighing 20,000 pounds. This artillery placements outside Yorktown, Virginia was shot by the most famous photographer of the War Mathew B. Brady (1822 –1896) .Best known for his portraits of celebrities and the documentation of the American Civil War. He is credited with being the father of photojournalism.

Batteria nr. 4 posta nei pressi di Yorktown con mortai da 13 La batteria nr. 4 era composta da 10 pezzi di mortai da 13 pollici ognuno del peso di 7,5 tonnellate ! Famoso scatto eseguito da Mathew B. Brady (1822-1896) nei pressi di Yorktown in Virginia. Molto conosciuto per i suoi ritratti di celebrità e per aver documentato tutta la Guerra Civile, Brady è considerato uno dei padri del fotogiornalismo.

◄ **Arlington, Va. Soldiers with 24-pdr. siege gun on wooden barbette carriage at Fort Corcoran**. From the serie of photographs of Washington, 1862-1865, view of the defenses of Washington.

Arlington, Virginia. Artiglieri nordisti con un pezzo d'assedio da 24-pdr. Montato su un supporto ruotato di legno a Fort Corcoran. Dalla serie delle foto dedicate alla difesa di Washington, 1862-1865.

◄ **Fair Oaks, Va., vicinity. Capt. James M. Robertson (third from left) and officers** in a photo of James F. Gibson. Regular artillerymen from Fitz John Porter's otherwise unengaged corps aided in the attack on Bloody Lane. Captain James Robertson led two batteries of the 2nd United States artillery in the assaults. He became a general after the war.

Fair Oaks, Virginia Il capitano James M. Robertson (terzo da sin.) e ufficiali in una foto di James F. Gibson. Appartenente al corpo di Fitz John Porter, fu impegnato nell'attacco a Bloody Lane. Il capitano Robertson comandò due batterie del 2° United States artillery nell'assalto. Dopo la guerra fu promosso generale.

▼ **Officers of 55th Inf. at Fort Tennalytown, D.C,** By Mathew Brady

Ufficiali del 55° fanteria a Fort Tennalytown, D.C, By Mathew Brady

▲ **City Point, Virginia. Negro soldier** guarding several 12-pdr. Napoleon. (Model 1857?) Near the railway.

City Point, Virginia. Un soldato di colore di guardia a numerosi cannoni Napoleon da 12pdr (Modello 1857?) Vicino alla ferrovia.

▶ **Lieutenant Colonel G.E. Chamberlain, 1st Vermont Artillery**

Il tenente colonnello G. G.E. Chamberlain, del 1° reggimento artiglieria del Vermont.

▶ **Savage Station, Va. Headquarters of Gen. George B. McClellan** on the Richmond & York River Railroad- Shot of George N. Barnard. 1862 June 27. Photograph from the main eastern theater of war, the Peninsular Campaign, May-August 1862

Savage Station, Virginia quartier generale del Gen. George B. McClellan nelle vicinanze Della ferrovia Richmond & York River. Foto di George N. Barnard. 27 giugno 1862. Foto dal principale teatro operativo Est della guerra .Campagna della penisola maggio agosto 1862.

Johnny Reb, the Confederate soldier

Johnny Reb, il soldato confederato

◄ Bernard Bluecher Graves, Corp., C.S.A.
This Confederate soldier joined the Hanover Artillery May 22, 1861. In Oct., 1862, he was transferred to the Amherst Artillery and fought with it the remainder of the war, a part of the time as a corporal. He was captured near Waynesboro, Va., Mar. 2, 1865 and imprisoned in Fort Delaware. He died at the age of forty-three. from an ambrotype by Rees & Brother, Richmond, Va.

Bernard Bluecher Graves, Caporale C.S.A. Questo soldato confederato si unì al Hanover Artillery il 22 maggio del 1861. nell'ottobre del 1862 venne trasferito al Amherst Artillery dove combattè per tutto il resto della guerra con il grado di caporale. venne poi catturato a Waynesboro, Va., il due marzo Del 1865 e imprigionato a Fort Delaware. Morì all'età di 43 anni. Da un ambrotipo di Rees & Brother, Richmond, Va.

◄ Three Confederate prisoners at Gettysburg, Pa. 1863 July.
Three Confederate enlisted men, tough and indipendent, captured at Gettysburg in one of the most famous shot of American Civil War. The last epic charge of Lee's army is just ended. They have lost the battle, and with it also the War... Probably they know it. They want record his unbowed performance before they await an hard future in a US prison.

Tre prigionieri confederati sul campo di battaglia di Gettysburg nel luglio del 1863.
Questa notissima immagine della Libreria del Congresso mostra tre fieri soldati sudisti appena catturati sul campo di Gettysburg. La battaglia, durata tre giorni si è chiusa con una sconfitta per il generale Lee. Insieme con la battaglia anche la Guerra ha ormai poco da offrire alle speranze del sud. Probabilmente questi indomiti prigionieri lo sanno, orgogliosamente offrono questa forte immagine prima di venire spediti in una triste prigione nordista.

► Capt. James S. West, C.S.A. Cavalry
Very retouched photos of rare complete image of a Confederate cavalry officer. Title from unverified information on negative sleeve.

Capitano James S.West della cavalleria confederata
Una foto assai ritoccata da un artista del tempo che ritrae una rara immagine di un ufficiale di cavalleria sudista. Le note sono ricavate da informazioni non verificate poste sul negativo.

◄ Portrait of Brig. Gen. Richard Lee Turberville Beale (1819 – 1893).

He was a Virginian lawyer, three-term United States Congressman from the Commonwealth of Virginia, and a brigadier general in the Confederate States Army during the American Civil War. Upon the secession of Virginia in 1861, Beale enlisted in the cavalry as a lieutenant. He was soon promoted to captain and then major. Later Beale was advanced to the rank of colonel and given command of the regiment, which included his sons. In March 1864, he made a forced march to intercept Union Col. Ulric Dahlgren (the son of the famous Admiral). His regiment of 9th Virginia Cavalry captured about 175 men and killed Dahlgren. The papers found upon Dahlgren's person, revealing a design to burn Richmond and kill President Jefferson Davis. These controversial papers discovered by Beale's troopers may have been a factor that influenced John Wilkes Booth in his decision to assassinate Abraham Lincoln. Later Beale was finally promoted to brigadier general.

Richard Lee Turberville Beale (1819 – 1893)
Era un uomo di legge e un eletto del congresso per la Virginia. Durante la Guerra Civile divenne anche generale. Dopo la secessione alla quale aderì prontamente, nel 1861 diventa tenente di cavalleria. Presto promosso capitano e poi maggiore, colonnello di un reggimento in cui militava anche un suo figlio e alla fine generale. Nel marzo del 1864 con le sue forze intercetta un raid nordista comandato dal colonnello nordista Ulric Dahlgren, (figlio del famoso ammiraglio inventore di cannoni. vedi foto a pag. 56). Nello scontro i suoi uomini catturano 175 nemici e uccidono il colonnello Dahlgren, al quale vengono trovati incartamenti che provano il piano federale di bruciare Richmond e uccidere il presidente confederato Jefferson Davis. E' probabile che queste carte influenzarono poi John Wilkes Booth nella sua decisione di assassinare Abraham Lincoln.

►George W.Custis Lee, Robert E. Lee, Walter Taylor at Richmond April 1865

The great Confederate commander , after Appomattox , in this famous image take on the porch of his Richmond home with Major general George Washington Curtis Lee (at left), and the Colonel Walter Taylor (At right). Custis Lee (1832-1913), was the eldest son of Robert E. Lee and Mary Anna Custis Lee. He served as a Confederate general in the American Civil War, primarily as an aide-de-camp to President Jefferson Davis, and succeeded his father as president of Washington and Lee University in Lexington, Virginia. Walter Herron Taylor (1838 –1916) was an American banker, lawyer, soldier, politician, author, and railroad executive from Norfolk, Virginia. During the American Civil War, he was an officer in the Confederate States Army, attaining the rank of lieutenant colonel as an aide to General Robert E. Lee.

George W.Custis Lee, Robert E. Lee e Walter Taylor a Richmond Aprile 1865
Il grande comandante sudista subito dopo Appomatox si fece fotografare in questa famosa immagine presa sul portico della sua casa di Richmond insieme con suo figlio, il generale G.W.C.Lee (a sinistra) e al colonnello Walter Taylor (a destra). Custis Lee (1832-1913) era il più vecchio dei figli di Lee e di Mary Custis Lee. Durante la Guerra servì come generale, aiutante di campo del presidente sudista Jefferson Davis. Dopo la morte del padre gli successe nella carica di presidente della Washington & Lee University di Lexington in Virginia. Walter Herron Taylor (1838-1916) fu un bancario, avvocato, soldato, politico, autore e dirigente ferroviario. Originario di Norfolk in Virginia, durante la Guerra ricoprì l'incarico di aiutante di campo del generale R.E.Lee.

◄ Portrait of Brig. Gen. John Sappington Marmaduke (1833 –1887) . He was a career military man and a West Point graduate. He is known for his service as a Confederate Major general during the American Civil War. Born into a political family, he later became the 25th Governor of Missouri from 1884 until his death in 1887.
During the Civil War he partecipate at several famous battles: Boonville, Shiloh, Prairie Grove, Springfield II, Hartville, battle of Cape Girardeau, Red River Campaign, Price's Raid and the battle of Mine Creek !

Ritratto del generale John Sappington Marmaduke (1833 –1887) militare di carriera, diplomato a West Point. Noto generale confederato. Nato in una famiglia di politici dopo la Guerra diventa il 25° governatore del Missouri dal 1884 fino al 1887 anno della sua scomparsa. Durante la Guerra Civile partecipa a tantissime battaglie: Boonville, Shiloh, Prairie Grove, Springfield II, Hartville, Cape Girardeau, campagna di Red River, Price's Raid ed infine la battaglia di Mine Creek.

► Unidentified soldier in Confederate uniform in 1861
A small image of the photographer Charles R.Ress of a Confederate soldier of Co. E, "Lynchburg Rifles," 11th Virginia Infantry Volunteers holding 1841 "Mississippi" rifle, Sheffield-type Bowie knife, canteen, box knapsack, blanket roll, and cartridge box.

Ritratto di un soldato confederato non identificato (1861)
Una piccola immagine da uso personale fatta dal fotografo Charles R.Ress del soldato sudista della compagnia E del reggimento "Lynchburg Rifles," 11° Virginia Infantry Volunteers armato di fucile Mississippi mod. 1841, coltellaccio di tipo Bowie, borraccia metallica, zaino, coperta arrotolata e giberna.

▲ **Six Confederate General officer. Bushrod Rust Johnson, (1817-1880).** He was one of a handful of Confederate generals who were born and raised in the North. **General Braxton Bragg (1817 –1876)** was a principal commander in the Western Theater of the American Civil War and later the military adviser to Confederate President Jefferson Davis. **Lieut. General William J. Hardee (1815 –1873)** was a career U.S. Army officer, serving during the Second Seminole War and fighting in the Mexican-American War. His pre-Civil War writings about military tactics were well known and widely used on both sides of the conflict. He is nicknamed "Old Reliable". **General Gustavus Woodson Smith, (1822-1896)** more commonly known as G.W. Smith, was a career United States Army officer who fought in the Mexican-American War, a civil engineer.He fought in the Battle of Seven Pines near Richmond during the Peninsula Campaign. **Maj. Gen. George E. Pickett (1825 – 1875)** was a career United States Army officer. He is best remembered for his participation in the futile and bloody assault at the Battle of Gettysburg that bears his name, Pickett's Charge. **General Bryan Grimes (1828 – 1880)** was a North Carolina plantation owner and a general officer. He fought in nearly all of the major battles of the Eastern Theater of that war.

Sei generali superiori dell'armata confederata. Bushrod Rust Johnson, (1817-1880). uno dei pochi generali sudisti nati al Nord. *General Braxton Bragg (1817-1876) fra i principali generali del fronte occidentale e consigliere militare del presidente Davis. Lieut. General William J. Hardee (1815-1873) militare di carriera, partecipò alle guerre coi Seminole e nella guerra Messicana. General Gustavus Woodson Smith, (1822-1896) combatté nella guerra Messico-Americana durante la guerra civile fu presente alla battaglia di Seven Pines in Virginia. Maj. Gen. George E. Pickett (1825-1875) militare di carriera, Ricordato per aver guidato la sanguinosa, inutile ma epica carica di Gettysburg che porta ancora oggi il suo nome. General Bryan Grimes (1828-1880) generale e latifondista della Carolina del Nord. Combatté in tutte le maggiori battaglie sul fronte est della Guerra.*

► **Major General James Ewell Brown (JEB) Stuart (1833-1864)**

Stuart was the most famous Confederate cavalry commander whose daring exploits made him a household name during the Civil War. During the Seven Days Battles in 1862, Stuart and his cavalry rode around the entire Union Army. At the age of 29, he became a Major General and took command of all of the cavalry in the Army of Virginia. Stuart's cavalry came to be feared throughout the Union ranks. The most dashing of all the *"beaux sabreurs"* of the Confederacy, was mortally wounded at the Battle of Yellow Tavern.

Major General James Ewell Brown (JEB) Stuart (1833-1864)
Stuart fu il più famoso comandante di cavalleria confederato e americano in generale. Durante la battaglia dei sette giorni nel 1862, Stuart fece continui raid micidiali dietro le linee unioniste. A soli 29 anni egli divenne generale in capo di tutta la cavalleria virginiana. La migliore delle "beaux sabreurs" confederate morì nella battaglia di Yellow Tavern.

◄ **Col. John S. Mosby, C.S.A.**

You are viewing a famous image that shows the Colonel John Singleton Mosby (1833-1916), nicknamed the "Gray Ghost", the famous Confederate Raider of the Civil War. He virtually invented Guerrilla Warfare, and as an old man, was friends with George S. Patton, who was a child. After the war, Mosby worked as an attorney and supported his former enemy's commander, President Ulysses S. Grant, serving as the U.S. consul to Hong Kong and in the Department of Justice.

Col. John S. Mosby, C.S.A.
quella che vedete è una foto nota del famoso raider confederato, il Colonnello John Singleton Mosby (1833-1916), soprannominato "Gray Ghost" (il fantasma grigio). Mosby fu in sostanza l'inventore della guerriglia. Dopo la guerra egli riprese l'attività di avvocato e ottenne dal suo nemico di una volta, il presidente Ulisse Grant, l'incarico di console americano ad Hong Kong. In tarda età fece anche amicizia con un bambino di nome George Patton...

▲ **Six Confederate General officer. John Bell Hood (1831-1879)** Confederate general for the Texas during the American Civil War. Hood had a reputation for bravery and aggressiveness that sometimes bordered on recklessness. **Joseph Wheeler (1836-1906)** has the rare distinction of serving as a general during war time for two opposing forces: first as a cavalry general in the Confederate States Army, and later as a general in the US Army during the Spanish-American War. **Benjamin Franklin Cheatham (1820-1886)** was a Tennessee aristocrat, California gold miner, and a Confederate General, serving in many battles of the Western Theater. **Beverly Holcombe Robertson (1827-1910)** was a cavalry officer in the United States Army on the Western frontier and later Confederate general in the major eastern battles. **Edmund Kirby Smith (1824-1893)** this great southern general was notable for his command of the Trans-Mississippi Department of the Confederacy after the fall of Vicksburg. **Benjamin Huger (1805-1877)** was a career United States Army ordnance officer who fought with distinction during the Mexican–American War. Later served as a Confederate general officer during the American Civil War.

Sei generali superiori dell'armata confederata. John Bell Hood (1831-1879) Generale adottato dal Texas, Hood ebbe una solida reputazione di coraggio e aggressività in battaglia. Joseph Wheeler (1836-1906) ebbe la curiosa caratteristica di combattere per due eserciti opposti, prima coi confederati e dopo la guerra con l'esercito americano nella guerra contro la Spagna. Benjamin Franklin Cheatham (1820-1886) aristocratico del Tennesse, cercatore d'oro in California e quindi generale sudista. Beverly Holcombe Robertson (1827-1910) generale di cavalleria prima nelle guerre di frontiera con l'US Army e poi sul teatro Ovest coi confederati. Edmund Kirby Smith (1824-1893) questo grande generale condusse con energia il fronte del Mississipi dopo la caduta di Vicksburg. Benjamin Huger (1805-1877) iniziò la carriera come militare d'ordinanza nella guerra messicano-americana e poi come generale confederato durante la Guerra Civile.

NAVAL WARFARE

La Guerra sul mare

◄ **David Glasgow Farragut (1801 –1870)** was the first rear admiral, vice admiral, and admiral in the United States Navy during the Civil War. He is remembered in popular culture for his order at the Battle of Mobile Bay, usually paraphrased: "Damn the torpedoes, full speed ahead!".

David Glasgow Farragut (1801 –1870) fu il primo e più importante ammiraglio E comandante navale americano durante la Guerra Civile Americana. Egli è ancor'oggi ricordato per IL suo atteggiamento durante la battaglia di Mobile Bay in cui disse:"accidenti I siluri, avanti tutta !".

▼ **Washington, D.C. Six marines with fixed bayonets at the Navy Yard 1864 April.** Photographs of the Federal Navy, and seaborne expeditions against the Atlantic Coast of the Confederacy.

Washington, D.C. Sei marines con baionetta innestata al Navy Yard nell'aprile 1864.
Foto della Federal Navy, sulla spedizione contro la costa atlantica della Confederazione.

◄ **Charleston Harbor, South Carolina. The rear Admiral John A. Dahlgren, here standing on deck of U.S.S. PAWNEE, near one of her massive pivot gun designed by himself.** John Adolphus Bernard Dahlgren (November 13, 1809 – July 12, 1870) was a United States Navy leader. He headed the Union Navy's ordnance department during the American Civil War and designed several different kinds of guns and cannons that were considered part of the reason the Union won the War. For these achievements, Dahlgren became known as the "father of American naval ordnance."
Baia di Charleston, South Carolina. L'ammiraglio John A.Dahlgren, fotografato sul ponte della nave della marina nordista U.S.S. Pawnee vicino ad uno dei suoi famosi cannoni da lui stesso creati. L'ammiraglio Dahlgren (13 novembre 1809-12 luglio 1870) fu un famoso comandante di marina. Egli fu messo alla guida del dipartimento d'ordinanza della marina durante la Guerra Civile. Dal suo ufficio elaborò tutta una serie di artiglierie e cannoni che a detta di molti furono, per la loro efficacia, una delle ragioni principali della vittoria unionista nella Guerra. Per tutti questi meriti, l'ammiraglio divenne noto come il "padre della potenza navale americana".

▲ **Morris Island, South Carolina. Naval Battery.** Two 80-pounder Whitworths guns and sailor crew. Breaching battery against Fort Sumpter at Morris Island July-August 1863. After the Confederates abandoned Morris Island in 1863, the Union occupied it and transferred many hundred Confederate officers from Fort Delaware to Morris Island. They were used as human shields in an attempt to silence the Confederate artillery at Fort Sumter and soon became known in the South as the Immortal Six Hundred.

Batteria navale piazzata a Morris Island South Carolina.
Una batteria navale composta da due cannoni Withworths di 80 pollici con i marinai in un attimo di pausa. I cannoni piazzati sull'isola dovevano far fuoco sulle difese confederate a Fort Sumter nell'estate del 1863. Dopo che i confederati furono costretti ad abbandonare l'isola, gli unionisti la occuparono e vi trasferirono centinaia di prigionieri sudisti da Fort Delaware per far si che con la loro presenza si dissuadesse dal tiro di controbatteria le difese confederate di Fort Sumter. Una sorta di scudi umani insomma, tanto che nel sud essi passarono alla storia col nome degli immortali seicento.

▶ **Beaufort, S.C. Gen. Isaac I. Stevens. 1862**
Photo of the Federal Navy, and seaborne expeditions against the Atlantic Coast of the Confederacy. Shot of T. O'Sullivan.
Beaufort, il Generale Isaac I. Stevens. 1862
Foto della marina federale, relativa alla spedizione contro la costa atlantica della confederazione. Scatto di T. O'Sullivan.

▲ **Six American Admiral of Union and Confederacy field. All works of photographer Brady. Commodore Franklin Buchanan, (1800-1874),** was an officer in the United States Navy who became the most famous admiral in the Confederate Navy during the American Civil War, and commanded the ironclad CSS Virginia. **Francis Hoyt Gregory (1789–1866)** was an officer in the United States Navy during the War of 1812 through to the Civil War, serving then as a Rear Admiral. **Richard Worsam Meade (1807-1870)** was an officer in the US Navy and was the brother of General George Meade, the victor of Gettysburg. **Matthew Fontaine Maury (1806 –1873)**, was a famous American astronomer, historian, oceanographer, meteorologist, cartographer, author, geologist, and educator. During Civil war as Virginian resigned his commission as a U.S. Navy commander and joined the Confederacy. **William David Porter (1808-1864)** was a flag officer of the United States Navy. He was also a foster brother of Admiral David Farragut. **David Dixon Porter (1813-1891)** was brother of William D. Porter . Porter helped improve the Navy as the Superintendent of the US Naval Academy after significant service in the American Civil War.

*Sei ammiragli e comandanti navali dell'Unione e della Confederazione ritratti da Brady. **Commodoro Franklin Buchanan, (1800-1874)**, già ufficiale della US Navy che divenne il più famoso ammiraglio sudista durante la guerra, fu anche comandante della CSS Virginia. **Francis Hoyt Gregory (1789–1866)** ufficiale della US Navy durante la guerra del 1812 e poi durante la Guerra Civile con il grado di contrammiraglio. **Richard Worsam Meade (1807-1870)** ufficiale della US Navy e fratello del più noto generale George Meade, il vincitore di Gettysburg. **Matthew Fontaine Maury (1806 –1873)**, famoso scienziato americano (astronomo, storico,cartografo, meteorologo, geologo ed educatore) , come virginiano allo scoppio delle ostilità lasciò l'incarico presso la US Navy e raggiunse la Confederazione. **William David Porter (1808-1864)** ufficiale della US Navy e fratellastro del grande ammiraglio Admiral David Farragut. **David Dixon Porter (1813-1891)** fratello di William D. Porter . Porter divenne sovrintendente dell'Accademia navale dopo il suo importante contributo fornito durante la Guerra Civile.*

▲ **Powder Monkey on U.S.S. Navy Ship.** An inspiring photograph of a Powder monkey by gun of U.S.S. New Hampshire, Federal depot ship off Charleston, South Carolina. 1864. This famous photo illustrates a very young man or boy leaning against cannon during the seaborne expeditions against the Atlantic Coast of the Confederacy, is one of the most famous of LC collection.

Powder Monkey a bordo di una nave unionista. Un'ispirata immagine di un Powder monkey da cannoni (letteralmente scimmia da polveri) della U.S.S. New Hampshire, presso il deposito federale di Charleston, South Carolina. 1864. La famosa immagine che ritrae un giovane ragazzo appoggiato ad un cannone nell'ambito delle operazioni navali contro la costa atlantica della Confederazione, è fra le più note della intera collezione della Library of Congress.

► **Officers of the USS Philadelphia before pilot-house.** Photographs of the Federal Navy, and seaborne expeditions against the Atlantic Coast of the Confederacy. Unknown location.

Ufficiali Della U.S.S Philadelphia in posa. Foto ripresa durante le operazioni contro la costa atlantica Della Confederazione.

▼ **Officers of the USS Monitor grouped by the turret.** Photo by J. F. Gibson, take the 1862 July 9 on James River, Virginia. From Photographs of the Federal Navy, and seaborne expeditions against the Atlantic Coast of the Confederacy.

Ufficiali Della U.S.S. Monitor in posa davanti alla torretta. Foto scattata il 9 luglio 1862 da J.F.Gibson sul fiume James in Virginia. Foto ripresa durante le operazioni contro la costa atlantica Della Confederazione.

Husbands, wives and children

Mogli, mariti e figli

◄ **John Hunt Morgan (1825-1864) and his wife.** Morgan is one of the leading Confederate raiders. in 1863, he and his men rode over 1,000 miles covering a region from Tennessee, up through Kentucky, into Indiana and on to southern Ohio. This would be the farthest north any uniformed Confederate troops penetrated during the war.

John Hunt Morgan (1825 – 1864) E moglie. Morgan fu un famoso raider confederato. Nel 1863, insieme coi suoi uomini percorse oltre 1.000 miglia in diversi stati del nord fra cui: Tennessee, Kentuchy, Indina ed Ohio. Fu la più grande penetrazione di truppe sudiste nel territorio dell'Unione di tutta la guerra.

▼ **G.A.Custer and his wife Elizabeth Bacon Custer (1842 1933)** . Elizabeth, after his death, she became an outspoken advocate for her husband's legacy through her popular books and lectures. Largely as a result of her endless campaigning on his behalf, Custer's iconic portrayal as the gallant fallen hero amid the glory of 'Custer's Last Stand' was a canon of American history for almost a century after his death.

G.A.Custer E sua moglie Elizabeth Bacon Custer (1842-1933). Elizabeth, dopo la morte del marito avvenuta al Little Big Horne, ne curò particolarmente il ricordo e l'immagine attraverso tutta una serie di pubblicazioni e interventi.

◄ **Maj. Gen. Abner Doubleday and his wife Mary.** Abner Doubleday (June 26, 1819 – January 26, 1893) was a career United States Army officer and Union general in the American Civil War. He fired the first unionist shot in defense of Fort Sumter, the opening battle of the War (the absolute first shot of the Civil War are of the Confederate Edmund Ruffin) and had a great role in the early fighting at the Battle of Gettysburg. Gettysburg was his most glorious day, but his relief by Maj. Gen. George G. Meade caused lasting enmity between the two men. Doubleday is often mistakenly credited with having invented baseball in the 1839, although he never made such a claim, and there is no evidence to support it. Here is with his wife Mary Hewitt married in 1852.

Il generale nordista Abner Doubleday ritratto con sua moglie Mary.
Abner Doubleday (1819-1893) fu un generale di carriera dell'esercito americano. Ebbe l'onore di sparare il primo colpo di fucile in difesa di Fort Sumter , nel corso della prima battaglia della Guerra (il primo colpo in assoluto della Guerra fu però sparato dal sudista Edmund Ruffin). Doubleday ebbe un ruolo importante durante la battaglia di Gettysburg, tuttavia screzi sorti con il generale Meade, comandante dell'armata nordista durante la battaglia provocarono la futura inimicizia fra i due. A Doubleday voci assegnano l'invenzione avvenuta nel 1839 del gioco del baseball, ma la cosa è ancora avvolta nel mistero e nella leggenda. In questa bella immagine lo vediamo con l'amatissima moglie Mary Hewitt sposata nel 1852.

◄ **Richmond, Virginia. Gen. Edward Otho Cresap Ord (1818-1883)**, wife and child at the residence of Jefferson Davis. In the doorway is the table on which the surrender of Gen. Robert E. Lee was signed. Ord was the designer of Fort Sam Houston, and a United States Army officer who saw action in the Seminole War, the Indian Wars, and the American Civil War. He commanded an army during the final days of the Civil War, and was instrumental in forcing the surrender of Confederate General Robert E. Lee.

Richmond, Virginia. Gen. Edward Otho Cresap Ord (1818-1883), con moglie e figlia nella residenza di Jefferson Davis. Sull'androne si vede il tavolino dove venne firmata la resa confederata da parte di Lee. Ord progettò Fort Sam Houston, e servì come ufficiale durante le guerre Indiane e Seminole. Durante la Guerra Civile comandò negli ultimi tempi un'armata con la quale ottenne la resa dei confederati da parte del generale Robert E. Lee.

◄ **City Point, Virginia. Brig. Gen. John A. Rawlins (1831-1869)** Chief of Staff, wife and child at Grant's headquarters." on the door of their quarters. Photograph from the main eastern theater of war, the siege of Petersburg, June 1864-April 1865.

City Point, Virginia. Brig. Gen. John A. Rawlins (1831-1869)Capo di Stato maggiore Del generale Grant, qui ritratto con moglie e sua figlia sulla porta dei loro alloggiamenti. Foto scattata nel teatro operativo orientale della guerra durante l'assedio di Petersburg, giugno 1864 - aprile 1865.

► **George Brinton McClellan (1826-1885) and his wife Ellen Mary Marcy McClellan**. He was one of the most important union general during the American Civil War. He organized the famous Army of the Potomac and served briefly (November 1861 to March 1862) as the general-in-chief of the Union Army.

George Brinton McClellan (1826-1885) ritratto con sua moglie Ellen Mary Marcy McClellan. Egli fu uno dei più noto generali federali durante la guerra. Organizzò la famosa armata del Potomac e per breve tempo (novembre 1861 - marzo 1862) fu comandante in capo dell'intera armata nordista.

◀ **Fredericksburg, Va. Nurses and officers of the U.S.** Sanitary Commission. Photo of James Gardner 1864 May 20. Photograph from the main eastern theater of war, Grant's Wilderness Campaign, May-June 1864.

Fredericksburg, Virginia. Nurses e personale del U.S. Sanitary Commission. Foto di James Gardner del 20 maggio 1864 per la serie relativa alla campagna di Wilderness del 1864.

▼ **District of Columbia.** In this bucolic pacific, image a relaxed Capt. Sellers and wife at Fort Totten. Smith, William Morris, photographer.

Distretto di Columbia. In questa pacifica e bucolica immagine vediamo rilassati, il capitano Sellers e moglie a Fort Totten. Fotografo: Smith, William Morris.

▲ **Brig. Gen. Charles Pomeroy Stone (1824-1887)**, and his daughter Hettie photographed together in the spring of 1863; Stone's USMA class ring can be seen on the little finger of his right hand. Stone was reportedly the first volunteer to enter the Union Army. Later he served in Egyptian army where he was given the rank of lieutenant general and the title of Ferik Pasha.

Brig. Gen. Charles Pomeroy Stone (1824-1887), e sua figlia Hettie fotografti nella primavera del 1863; nella mano destra Stone tiene la medaglia del USMA class ring.Stone è ricordato come il primo volontario nell'armata unionista. Questo colorito personaggio più tardi si arruolò nell'esercito egiziano dove raggiunse il grado di generale comandante ed il titolo di Ferik Pascià.

◀ **Unidentified soldier in Union sergeant's frock coat** and forage cap with unidentified woman in dress and hat with veil. *Sergente nordista non identificato con accanto probabilmente sua moglie in abito elegante, capello e velo.*

Curiosity & Miscellaneous
Varie e curiose

◄ **Edwin Chamberlain** of Company G, 11th New Hampshire Infantry Regiment in sergeant's uniform with guitar

Edwin Chamberlain compagnia del 11° New Hampshire Infantry Regiment in uniforme con gradi da sergente mentre suona la chitarra.

◄ **Integrated black and white boys "Soldier group, Federal Army."** Circa 1865 location and photographer unknown.

Ragazzini bianchi e neri integrati nell'esercito nordista. 1865 circa località e fotografo sconosciuti.

► **Soldier Reading Letter.** Fort Brady, Virginia 1864; Three officers of the 1st Connecticut Heavy Artillery.

Soldati che leggono lettere. Fort Brady, Virginia. Tre ufficiali del 1° Connecticut Artiglieria pesante.

▲ **Antietam, Maryland (vicinity). Maj. Allan Pinkerton,** Secret Service Department and friends. A famous shot of Alexander Gardner, friend of Pinkerton. October 1862.

Antietam, Maryland (prossimità). Il maggiore Allan Pinkerton, responsabile del Secret Service Department insieme ad amici poliziotti con indubbia aria da "sbirri". Un famoso scatto di Alexander Gardner, amico dello stesso Pinkerton. Ottobre1862.

◄ **February 1863. Captain J.W. Forsyth**, provost marshal, Aquia Creek, Virginia. An army marches on its stomach, and the stomach's boots are made of dough. Or something like that…

Febbraio 1863 il Capitano J.W. Forsyth, responsabile dell'intendenza ad Aquia Creek, in Virginia. Un esercito marcia solo se ha lo stomacopieno, e gli stivali dello stomaco sono fatti di pasta, o qualcosa del genere…

▲**Embalming surgeon at work on soldier's body.**
Before the Civil War, embalming was performed mainly
to preserve the body for the purpose of medical studies.
This practice become popular in the United States until
the Civil War, when there was a need to preserve the dead
for the long journey home. If a body wasn't embalmed
properly, legally it couldn't be transported, and often it
would end up buried in a shallow grave on the battlefield…
Unknown location and photographer, 1863 about.

Medico imbalsamatore al lavoro sul corpo di un soldato.
Prima della Guerra Civile, l'imbalsamazione era effettuata
solo per studi scientifici. Questa pratica divenne diffusa
proprio durante gli anni della guerra per permettere ai
corpi dei caduti di arrivare alle loro case dopo lunghi
viaggi in condizioni "presentabili" ed evitare cosi di
essere seppelliti in tombe vicine al campo di battaglia.
Località e fotografo sconosciuti. Foto fatta nel 1863 circa.

▶ **Lunch for two photographers at Bull Run**,
Virginia, winter 1862-63. near Ruins of railroad
bridge at Blackburn's Ford.
Il pasto dei fotografi a Bull Run, Virginia, inverno 1862-63.
Vicino alle rovine Del ponte ferroviario a Blackburn's Ford.

▲General Belknap and aides. William Worth Belknap (1829-1890) was a US Army general, government administrator, and United States Secretary of War. He was the only Cabinet secretary ever to have been impeached by the United States House of Representatives.

Il Generale Belknap e aiutanti. William Worth Belknap (1829-1890) fu un generale nordista, politico e Segretario della Guerra. Fu anche il solo e unico segretario che sia stato messo sotto accusa dalla camera dei rappresentanti degli USA.

▶ **Gen. Ambrose E. Burnside (reading newspaper) with Mathew B. Brady (nearest tree)** at Army of the Potomac headquarters. Ambrose Everett Burnside (1824-1881) was an American soldier, railroad executive, inventor, industrialist, and politician. As a Union Army general in the American Civil War, he conducted successful campaigns in North Carolina and East Tennessee but was defeated in the disastrous Battle of Fredericksburg and Battle of the Crater. His distinctive style of facial hair is now known as sideburns, derived from his last name.

Il Gen. Ambrose E. Burnside (che legge un giornale) con Mathew B. Brady (vicino l'albero) al quartier generale dell'armata del Potomac. Ambrose Everett Burnside (1824-1881) era un soldato americano, un impresario ferroviario, inventore, industriale e politico. Come generale dell'Unione durante la Guerra Civile, ottenne importanti successi nel North Carolina e nel Tennessee ma fu pesantemente sconfitto nella battaglia di Fredericksburg e in quella successiva del Cratere. Il suo caratteristico stile di tenere i capelli era denominato sideburns (basettone), nomignolo che era un anagramma del suo cognome.

◀ **Arrival of a wagon of Negro family in the lines**

L'arrivo di un vagone con una famiglia di colore dietro le linee

▶ **Zouave ambulance crew** demonstrating removal of wounded soldiers from the field.

Personale zuavo di un ambulanza militare in una dimostrazione di rimozione feriti dal campo di battaglia.

▲ **Washington Navy Yard, D.C. Lewis Payne, in sweater, seated and manacled.** By A. Gardner, photographer of the assassination of Pres. Lincoln's trial. This photograph has background of dark metal, and was presumably taken on the monitors, USS Montauk and Saugus, where the conspirators were for a time confined.

Washington Navy Yard, D.C. Lewis Payne, seduto e ammanettato. Foto di A. Gardner, che riprese tutti i protagonisti dell'assassinio del Presidente Lincoln. Sullo sfondo della foto la parete metallica della nave monitor, USS Montauk & Saugus, sulla quale i cospiratori vennero trattenuti per qualche tempo.

AFTERMATH

Dopo la Guerra

◄ **C.S.A. Veterans, Sgt. J.J. Dackett,** Co. I. 3rd S.C.V., wearing hat with bullet holes received in the Battle of Chickamauga Sept. 20, 1863, Photo shows the Gettysburg Reunion (the Great Reunion) of July 1913. At the time of the seventy-fifth anniversary of the Battle of Gettysburg and of the Reunion of Confederate and Union Veterans, July 1-4, 1938, nearly 8,000 participants in the Civil War were still living. Of these, 1,845 attended the reunion.

Il veterano sergente confederato J.J. Dackett, indossa il cappello con cui ricevette un colpo di moschetto che lo forò, alla battaglia di Chickamauga del 20 settembre 1863, Foto ripresa all'adunata del cinquantenario di Gettysburg (the Great Reunion) del luglio 1913. Al tempo della successiva riunione, ricorrenti i 75 anni della battaglia, nel luglio del 1938 sopravvivevano ancora circa 8.000 partecipanti alla grande battaglia e di questi ben 1.845 parteciparono all'evento.

◄ **This photo shows a moment of the Gettysburg Reunion** (the Great Reunion) of July 1913, which commemorated the 50th anniversary of the battle. Two veterans seated on steps and shaking hands; one has his arm on shoulder of the other.

Foto ripresa nel luglio del 1913 in occasione del cinquantenario della battaglia di Gettysburg (the Great Reunion). Due veterani seduti sui gradini con le mani tremanti ma lo sguardo fiero, uno il sudista ha il suo braccio sulla spalla dell'altro (nordista).

► **Daniel Edgar Sickles (1819 – 1914)** was a Union general in the American Civil War. At the Battle of Gettysburg, he insubordinately moved his III Corps to a position in which it was virtually destroyed, an action that continues to generate controversy. His combat career ended the same days at Gettysburg when his leg was struck by cannon fire. Here he is at Gettysburg battlefield during the Great Reunion of 1913.

Daniel Edgar Sickles (1819 – 1914). Fu un generale nordista durante la guerra civile, personaggio controverso (uccise l'amante di sua moglie). A Gettysburg mosse il proprio 3° Corpo in una posizione critica e venne insubordinato. Sempre a Gettysburg, giornata decisiva per Sickles, egli perse una gamba stroncata da un colpo di cannone. In questa foto lo vediamo firmare autografi durante la Great Reunion sul campo di battaglia di Gettysburg del 1913.

▲ **1-4 July 1913 Oldest Confederate veterans** and family at the Great Reunion on Gettysburg battlefield

*1-4 luglio 1913, **vecchi veterani** dell'armata confederata con familiari presenti alla Great Reunion sul campo di battaglia di Gettysburg.*

◄ **John Lawrence Burns** was born in Burlington, New Jersey, of Scottish ancestry (1793 –1872), veteran of the War of 1812. He served as an enlisted man, fighting in numerous battles, including Lundy's Lane, and volunteered for both the Mexican-American War became a 70-year-old civilian combatant with the Union Army at the Battle of Gettysburg during the American Civil War. He was wounded, but survived to become a national celebrity.

John Lawrence Burns nacque a Burlington, New Jersey, di famiglia d'origine scozzese (1793 –1872), veterano della guerra del 1812. Prese parte a numerose battaglie,inclusa quella di Lundy's Lane, fu anche volontario nella guerra contro il Mexico. A 70 anni divenne il più anziano combattente dell'armata nordista. Presente a Gettysburg durante la Guerra Civile, egli rimase ferito ma sopravvisse diventando una celebrità nazionale.

**▲▶ Again two images of Veterans'
reunion on Civil War battlefields**

At the time of the seventy-fifth
anniversary of the Battle of Gettysburg
and of the Reunion of Confederate and
Union Veterans, July 1-4, 1938, nearly
8,000 participants in the Civil War were
still living. Of these, 1,845 attended
the reunion. Union and Confederate
veterans (right) are here shown clasping
hands across the stone wall.

*Altre due immagini delle riunioni di
veterani Della Guerra Civile. Al tempo
della Great Reunion del luglio 1938, si
calcola che fossero ancora in vita circa
8.000 partecipanti della Guerra Civile,
di questi ben 1.845 si presentarono alla
riunione sul campo di Gettysburg. A
destra una immagine di tale incontro
che mostra due veterani che 70 anni
dopo si stringono la mano.*

IMPORTANT EVENTS DURING THE AMERICAN CIVIL WAR

1861

April 12	Confederate troops attacked Fort Sumter.
April 15 -19	Lincoln issued a call for troops. Lincoln proclaimed a blockade of the South.
May 21	Richmond, Virginia, chosen as the Confederate capital.
July 21	Northern troops retreated in disorder after the First Battle of Bull Run (Manassas).

1862

Feb. 6	Fort Henry fell to Union forces.
Feb. 16	Grant's troops captured Fort Donelson.
March 9	The ironclad ships Monitor and Merrimack (Virginia) battled to a draw.
April 6-7	Both sides suffered heavy losses in the Battle of Shiloh, won by the Union.
April 16	The Confederacy began to draft soldiers.
April 18-25	Farragut attacked and captured New Orleans.
May 4	McClellan's Union troops occupied Yorktown, Virginia, and advanced on Richmond.
May 30	Northern forces occupied Corinth, Mississippi.
June 6	Memphis fell to Union armies.
June 25-July 1	Confederate forces under Lee saved Richmond in the Battles of the Seven Days.
Aug. 27-30	Lee and Jackson led Southern troops to victory in the Second Battle of Bull Run (Manassas).
Sept. 17	Confederate forces retreated in defeat after the bloody Battle of Antietam (Sharpsburg).
Oct. 8	Buell's forces ended Bragg's invasion of Kentucky in the Battle of Perryville.
Dec. 13	Burnside's Union forces received a crushing blow in the Battle of Fredericksburg.
Dec. 31	Union troops under Rosecrans forced the Confederates to retreat after the Battle of Stones River

1863

Jan. 1	Lincoln issued the Emancipation Proclamation.
May 1-4	Northern troops under Hooker were defeated in the Battle of Chancellorsville.
May 1-19	Grant's army defeated the Confederates in Mississippi and began to besiege Vicksburg.
July 1-3	The Battle of Gettysburg ended in a Southern defeat and marked a turning point in the war.
July 4, 8	Vicksburg fell to Northern troops. Northern forces occupied Port Hudson, Louisiana.
Sept. 19-20	Southern troops under Bragg won the Battle of Chickamauga.
Nov. 19	Lincoln delivered the Gettysburg Address.
Nov. 23-25	Grant and Thomas led Union armies to victory in the Battle of Chattanooga.

1864

March 9	Grant became general in chief of the North.
May 5-6	Union and Confederate troops clashed in the Battle of the Wilderness.
May 8-19	Grant and Lee held their positions in the Battle of Spotsylvania Court House.
June 3	The Union suffered heavy losses on the final day of the Battle of Cold Harbor.
June 20	Grant's troops laid siege to Petersburg, Virginia.
July 11-12	Early's Confederate forces almost reached Washington but retreated after brief fighting.
Aug. 5	Farragut won the Battle of Mobile Bay.
Sept. 2	Northern troops under Sherman captured Atlanta.
Sept. 19-Oct. 19	Sheridan led his troops on a rampage of destruction in the Shenandoah Valley.
Nov. 8	Lincoln was reelected president.
Nov. 15	Sherman began his march through Georgia.
Nov. 23	Hood invaded Tennessee.
Nov. 30	Schofield's Union forces inflicted heavy losses on Hood in the Battle of Franklin.
Dec. 15-16	The Battle of Nashville smashed Hood's army.
Dec. 21	Sherman's troops occupied Savannah, Georgia.

1865

Feb. 6	Lee became general in chief of the South.
April 2	Confederate troops gave up Petersburg and Richmond.
April 9	Lee surrendered to Grant at Appomattox.
April 14	Lincoln was shot. He died the following morning.
April 26 –May 4	Johnston surrendered to Sherman. Confederate forces in Alabama and Mississippi surrendered.
May 11 -26	Jefferson Davis was captured. The last Confederate troops surrendered.

BIBLIOGRAPHY - BIBLIOGRAFIA

- Mathew Brady & Image of history by M.Panzer, Publisher: Smithsonian 1997
- Mr. Lincoln's Camera Man: Mathew B. Brady by R.Meredith, Dover Publications 1974
- Russell's Civil War Photographs (Dover Photography Collections 1982) by A.Russell
- Photo by Brady: A Picture of the Civil War by J. Armstrong . Atheneum (2005)
- Matthew B. Brady by W, Youngblood. Chartwell Books, Inc. (2008)
- Brady's Civil War Journal Photographing the War 1861-1865 by T.P.Savas Skyhorse Pub.2008
- Eyewitness to the Civil War by S. Hyslop. National Geographic, (2006)
- The Civil War: A Visual History . DK Publishing (2011)
- In the Wake of Battle: The Civil War Images of Mathew Brady by G.Sullivan Prestel Pub 2004
- Touched by Fire: A National Historical Society Photographic Portrait of the Civil War by W.Davis . Black Dog & Leventhal Publishers (1997)
- Gardner's Photographic Sketchbook of the Civil War by A.Gardner Dover Pub. 1959
- On Alexander Gardner's Photographic Sketch Book of the Civil War by A.W.Lee, 2008
- Photographic Views of Sherman's March by G.N.Barnard Dover Pub. 2009
- The Library of Congress Civil War Desk Ref. by M.E.Wagner. Simon & Schuster 2009
- Civil War Curiosities: Strange Stories, Oddities, Events, and Coincidences by W.Garrison Thomas Nelson; Reprint. Edition 2000
- Fields of Honor: Pivotal Battles of the Civil War by E.C.Bearss. National Geographic 2007
- Brady's Civil War: A Collection of Memorable Civil War Images Photographed by Mathew Brady and His Assistants. By W.Garrison Lyons Press; Revised edition (2011)
- The Big Book of the Civil War: Fascinating Facts about the Civil War, Including Historic Photographs, Maps, and Documents By J.Mattern. Running Press (2007)
- The Civil War: Strange & Fascinating Facts by B.Davis. Wings Pub. (1988)
- The Fighting men of the Civil War by W.Davis, Salamander book 1989.
- The Battlefields of Civil War by W.Davis, Salamander book 1989.
- The Commanders of the Civil War by W.Davis, Salamander book 1989.
- Billy Yank the uniform of the Union Army 1861-1865 by M.McAfee. Grenhill book 1996
- Johnny Reb the uniform of the Confederate Army 1861-1865 by L.Jensen Grenhill 1996
- Leaders of the North and South by B.Sell. Metrobooks 1996
- Naval Warfare by John C.Wideman. Metrobooks 1997
- Crucial land battles by David Phillips. Metrobooks 1996
- Maps of the Civil War by David Phillips. Metrobooks 1998
- Regiments and uniforms of the Civil War by Don Troiani. Stackpole Books 2002
- Civil War by Don Troiani. Stackpole Books 1995
- Images of the Civil war by M.Kunstler and J.McPherson. Gramercy books 1992.
- Civil War days by J.Bowen . New Burlington books 1987
- Combat uniforms of the Civil war by M.Lloyd. Brian Tood pub 1990

Libri in Italiano

- Storia Della Guerra Civile Americana di Raimondo Luraghi. BUR Rizzoli 1994
- 5 lezioni sulla Guerra Civile Americana di Raimondo Luraghi. La città del sole 1997
- La Guerra Civile Americana di B.Catton. Edizioni Cepim 1975

TITOLI PUBBLICATI - ALREADY PUBLISHING

WWW.SOLDIERSHOP.COM   WWW.BOOKMOON.COM